®

D1076619

your toddler's development

your toddler's development
caroline deacon

Launched in 1938, the **teach yourself** series grew rapidly in response to the world's wartime needs. Loved and trusted by over 50 million readers, the series has continued to respond to society's changing interests and passions and now, 70 years on, includes over 500 titles, from Arabic and Beekeeping to Yoga and Zulu. What would you like to learn?

be where you want to be with **teach yourself**

For UK order enquiries: please contact Bookpoint Ltd, 130 Milton Park, Abingdon, Oxon OX14 4SB. Telephone: +44 (0) 1235 827720. Fax: +44 (0) 1235 400454. Lines are open 09.00–17.00, Monday to Saturday, with a 24-hour message answering service. Details about our titles and how to order are available at www.teachyourself.co.uk

Long renowned as the authoritative source for self-guided learning – with more than 50 million copies sold worldwide – the **teach yourself** series includes over 500 titles in the fields of languages, crafts, hobbies, business, computing and education.

British Library Cataloguing in Publication Data: a catalogue record for this title is available from the British Library.

First published in UK 2008 by Hodder Education, part of Hachette Livre UK, 338 Euston Road, London, NW1 3BH.

This edition published 2008.

The **teach yourself** name is a registered trademark of Hodder Headline.

Copyright © 2008 Caroline Deacon

Typeset by Transet Limited, Coventry, England.
Printed in Great Britain for Hodder Education, an Hachette Livre UK Company, 338 Euston Road, London NW1 3BH, by Cox & Wyman Ltd, Reading, Berkshire.

The publisher has used its best endeavours to ensure that the URLs for external websites referred to in this book are correct and active at the time of going to press. However, the publisher and the author have no responsibility for the websites and can make no guarantee that a site will remain live or that the content will remain relevant, decent or appropriate.

The logging and manufacturing processes are expected to conform to the environmental regulations of the country of origin.

Hachette Livre UK's policy is to use papers that are natural, renewable and recyclable products and made from wood grown in sustainable forests. The logging and manufacturing processes are expected to conform to the environmental regulations of the country of origin.

Impression number   10 9 8 7 6 5 4 3 2 1
Year   2012 2011 2010 2009 2008

contents

dedication

To my nephews and nieces: Alice, Poppy, Ollie, Benjamin and Christie.

01

introduction – the birth of a toddler

In this chapter you will learn:

- how your toddler's brain has developed so far and the significance of this
- what your role is in parenting your toddler
- how parenting a toddler impacts on you
- how this book works and what it can do for you.

Congratulations! You have survived that critical time of transition to parenthood, have looked after a baby and survived. Really it would only be fair if life could settle down now and become easier after those early months, but no, your baby is now turning into a toddler, and presenting you with a whole new set of challenges. You may indeed be an expert in parenting your baby, but unfortunately your child is no longer that baby, and you are now a novice again, wondering where the instruction manual is this time. While this book may not be able to tell you where the on/off switch is, it will hopefully explain why your baby has morphed into this stranger, why he behaves as he does, and offer you some suggestions on how to cope. It will also help you understand your role in aiding this small person to develop into a bigger, more rounded, more secure and more intelligent person.

The birth of a toddler

It's quite a sobering thought to consider that as your baby gets moving and officially becomes a toddler, despite the fact you have had him around for several months, if he were the offspring of any other species, he would only just be born. Extrapolating from other species, scientists have worked out that human babies are born about nine months too early. Yes, that pregnancy, which seemed to go on forever as it was, should really have lasted 18 months!

Our species is the most successful one on the planet for two reasons: firstly because we are intelligent and can problem-solve, reason and make tools; and secondly because we can adapt to the environment we find ourselves in – be it arctic or tropics, we can survive.

Intelligence requires a big brain and therefore a big head, but walking upright on two legs to leave our hands free for making tools means having a narrow pelvis, and immediately as you can see, there is a conflict. How could we give birth to babies with big heads and still walk upright? The answer is to give birth to premature babies, and thus our babies are born nine months too early.

Yet despite the fact that being born early is risky, as babies are incredibly vulnerable, being born early also helps in that second success strategy, adapting to the environment, and thus our babies' brains do most of their growing in their particular environment, thereby moulding themselves to cope with a diet of fruit, fish or whale-meat, to speak Japanese or English, to be emotionally inhibited with a 'stiff upper lip' or uninhibited and emotionally volatile.

How your toddler's brain develops

So your toddler was born nine months early, but this means he can adapt to his environment. Because his brain does most of its growing outside the womb, it grows in response to what is needed.

In the first year of life, your toddler's brain doubled in size to become half the size it will be as an adult. By the time he is three years old, his brain will be three-quarters its final size. It is also a very busy brain! At age two, his brain uses the same amount of energy as yours does even though it is only half the size of yours, and at age three it will use twice the energy of yours. It will stay this busy until he is about nine or ten years of age, when it gradually reduces to reach adult levels around age 18.

Why is your toddler's brain so busy? It's setting up connections. At birth each neuron (brain cell) has around 2,500 synapses (connections) and these increase in number rapidly, reaching a peak at around two to three years of age when there are about 15,000 synapses per neuron, more than are present in the adult brain. So even though all the neurons he will ever need are present at birth, the changes in the size of his brain are to do with growing and making connections. As a connection is used it strengthens and grows, pushing the neurons apart. After age three, your toddler's brain starts deleting all the connections which are not used, while the ones that carry the most messages get stronger and survive. You could think of your toddler as one big potential. All those connections waiting to be used, to be strengthened by experience, or pruned when not needed. In fact it sounds quite frightening to consider that children lose about 20 billion synapses per day between early childhood and adolescence. It is this pruning throughout time which means children become less flexible and creative, less suggestible but also become more efficient, able to remember things, to recall them efficiently, and to become self-aware.

Thus when a baby is born, he is incredibly adaptable; his brain can take him in whichever direction is needed. If one part of his brain is damaged then another part can take over. If something is not needed it can be deleted, allowing that part of the brain to be used for something else. Deaf children, for instance, use the part of the brain that would normally become the auditory cortex to process visual information instead. If you live in an environment with lots of horizontal and vertical lines (like a city) you get better at spotting things that are horizontal and vertical, whereas if you were raised in Northern America in a tepee, as are Canadian Indian babies, then you would be better at seeing oblique orientations. If you live in Yorkshire you become acutely attuned to Yorkshire vowels, being able to tell whether the speaker comes from your own county or from Lancashire, Northumberland or the Midlands, and although you would recognize words spoken in an American accent as being English, you would not be able to tell the difference between a New Yorker, Texan or Californian.

Why you are important to your toddler

During the first year of your toddler's life, his brain was wiring up in response to his environment, and this shaping continues through these formative toddler years. Even though your toddler will not remember much, if anything at all, from these early years, you are incredibly important in moulding this individual at this age. Never again will you have so much influence on a person! You are literally creating a human being through the way you interact with him.

What your toddler needs is lots of consistency. You will find yourself repeating things over and over again, but this is what he needs. He is also experimenting with you, pushing at boundaries, trying to establish what he can and cannot do, what the world expects from him.

Nowadays we have a choice, and you can choose what kind of parent you want to be, how you want your family life to be. Some people like a real sense of order and routine, some like to be more spontaneous. But perhaps now is a good time to take stock of your life, consider what is really important now that you are a family, because your values will be imbedded in your child.

It is quite important that you and your partner take time together to talk about your attitudes, your feelings about behaviour, and really work out what values you want to impart to your children over these formative years. Of course your children will do what you do, not what you say, so you may need to make changes in your own lifestyles. For instance, if you want your children to value mealtimes and sit at a table to eat, you cannot then take your own food on a tray in front of the TV! If you want them to talk respectfully to you and to other adults, you will have to model this in your own behaviour.

Having decided what is important, you might also need to think about what is not so important, and what you will choose to ignore, for the time being anyway. You don't want to be always saying 'no!'

How parenting a toddler feels

Having recovered from that massive, life-changing experience of becoming a parent, having finally recovered from the birth and subsequent exhaustion of feeding a baby day and night, seeing your baby's personality emerge and his interest in the world develop, perhaps to a point where life began to feel calm and you felt in control again, your baby turns into a toddler, and suddenly you are back in stress mode again, as he throws new challenges at you.

As toddlerhood progresses, your child can seem very physical, needing to explore and try everything. Incapable of waiting, he needs immediate gratification. In some ways it feels as if he has turned against you. He rages against you and you can do nothing right. At other times you realize that you are still his 'hero'. He wants to imitate and join in everything you are doing. Living with this physical and emotional whirlwind can be immensely tiring. Make sure you make time for yourself too, to recuperate your energy. If you are at home full-time with your child, make sure you get regular time off; after all, no other job demands a seven-day week commitment, and neither should parenting. If you are at work, then no doubt you want to spend as much time as possible with your toddler to make up for this, but you also need time to yourself to recharge your own batteries.

The other big source of conflict with a toddler is our different speeds of doing things. Toddlers are simply incapable, for instance, of walking for long distances in a straight line. They have no sense of wanting to get somewhere, they prefer to enjoy where they are. When you are with your child, your pace of life needs to slow right down. To avoid feeling frustrated, plan your day with lots of leeway, and always be flexible. Does it matter if it takes an hour to post a letter? This era, of dawdling, of stopping to explore every new thing, won't last long and should be savoured before you are both forever dashing to meet deadlines, school times etc.

- When you are with your toddler, go at his pace and let him drive the agenda, but make sure you are really fully present.
- This also means making sure you have time in the week when you are not with your toddler, time off to do your own thing and disengage your brain.
- If you need to get somewhere with your toddler, allow at least twice as long as you would normally do.
- You can win battles with your toddler because you are bigger and stronger than he is, but this is a hollow victory. Far better to interact positively with your toddler, and this means understanding why he behaves the way he does and adapting your life to his needs as far as is possible.

Changing emotions

Your toddler may cling to you on occasions in the same way that young monkeys cling to their mother's fur for safety and reassurance. As he learns to talk, and can tell you how he feels, he will cling less, but his need for physical reassurance will fluctuate off and on until he becomes an adult. As you will see, particularly in Chapter 06, a clingy toddler does not mean an insecure toddler; indeed the fact that he does cling to you indicates that he is more secure in his love for you than a toddler who might seem indifferent.

On the other hand, love is on his terms; he will not see that you might have any want or need for a cuddle yourself – being able to see the world from your point of view will not be possible until he is older (see Chapter 21). It can feel distressing when your baby now refuses a cuddle, wriggling away. You need to be ready with cuddles without forcing them on him – not always easy!

How this book works

The purpose of this book is for you to understand how your toddler is developing, and what you can do to help this development. Understanding this will also help you to understand why he behaves the way he does. Because parents of toddlers often find themselves grappling with behaviour issues, unable to raise their heads and see beyond the tantrums and the food fights, the book starts with a section called 'The issues' where we consider the main behaviour issues, why they happen and what you can do about them.

After this we get into the more fun stuff; looking at how your toddler actually develops and what you can do to help. The first part looks at your how your toddler fits into the world; his role in the family, how he becomes emotionally secure and socially aware. We will have already looked at this briefly in the 'issues' section, but here there is more time to look at helping your child become an emotionally and socially settled human being.

We then look at your toddler's creative and intellectual development. Eventually he will grow up into an intelligent human being, capable of all sorts of rational, abstract and creative thinking; how does he get there? As a toddler, he develops his intellect mostly through play, and this section looks at all the different types of play, what they do for your child, and what you need to do to help. We also look at the role of TV, computer and indeed formal education in your toddler's intellectual and creative development.

Finally we look at how he actually organizes his brain into an intelligent tool; how he builds up knowledge, how he recalls or remembers it, and how he learns to speak, and what this means for his developing intelligence.

The book ends with a section on special developmental situations which may become of interest to you at this stage – issues like autism, ADHD and dyslexia, as well as giving you more information and resources if you want to take any of this information further.

Given that time is probably the one thing you don't have, you should be able to dip in and out of sections as needed, and hopefully find quick answers to your queries. But above all, the hope is that this book will provide you with plenty of ideas to help you enjoy life with a toddler to the full.

Summary of this chapter

- Babies are born nine months too early, which allows them to develop in response to their environment.
- Your toddler's brain is incredibly busy, making connections in response to the world in which he lives.
- You are therefore incredibly influential in moulding your toddler into the person he will become.
- Today parents can choose how they want to parent, so it is important that you make time to talk through the way you want to be.
- Parenting a toddler is very tiring, so you must make time to recharge your own batteries.

section one

parenting the toddler – the issues

Introduction

This section is for those who are having problems right now with their toddler and who need some immediate, practical solutions. We start by looking at why toddlers can be difficult in the first place, what is happening in their brains, the conflicts they are experiencing and how to handle difficult behaviour. We also look at why you may be having conflicts over diet, toilet training and sleep and what to do about these common battles. Even if you are not having problems now, you might want to read this section so you can gain an understanding of what drives your child, and what may occur for you in the future. You can also dip into these chapters at any time as and when they become relevant.

02

what's the problem with toddlers?

In this chapter you will learn:
- why toddlers are in conflict
- what tantrums mean and what to do about them
- how to set boundaries and maintain them.

It sometimes seems to happen overnight; your smiling, amenable baby turns into a small, mobile person who rages against you and the world, throwing tantrums at the slightest thing, doing exactly what you don't want her to do, and unable to control herself. She is miserable, you are miserable – and everyone else just says, 'Oh it's the terrible twos'. What has happened?

The mobile toddler in conflict

As your toddler becomes mobile, she is in conflict. Now she can rush off and really explore this world but, in so doing, she is of course in danger of eating something poisonous, or being eaten by a sabre tooth tiger. Well, perhaps not in the twenty-first century developed world, but as far as her genetic inheritance is concerned, all her ancestors, up until a few seconds ago in evolutionary terms, were in those kinds of danger, and so we can presume that there must be some ancient survival mechanism which will kick in to protect her.

We are guessing here, but it seems logical to assume that your toddler is going to be feeling pushed and pulled – wanting to explore but being fearful about what will happen if she explores the wrong thing. Her safety net here is you and ideally you would be keeping a watchful eye on her 24/7, letting her do whatever she wants to satisfy that urge to explore and experiment, only stopping her when she is in actual physical danger. Unfortunately, although you do sometimes grab her when she is in immediate danger, we adults also seem to be thwarting her when there is no obvious danger, and as a result, your child is confused and feels restricted, raging against your inexplicable and inconsistent behaviour.

Testing beliefs – the experimenting toddler

The other big issue for your toddler was that until recently, she did not really realize that she was a person distinct from you; it is only at around eight months that she comes to understand that people continue to exist when she can't see them, and that you are a separate person.

Even though she now grasps that concept (which psychologists refer to as object permanence) she has still some way to go before she can understand that people can have different viewpoints from her own, that they can see the world in different ways, feel differently about different things and so on. We will look at how this understanding develops in the chapter on the development of mind (Chapter 21) but suffice to say at this point that during the early toddler years, your child is only just beginning to understand that you might see the world in a different way, that you may have different beliefs, desires and opinions, and this idea is completely fascinating to her.

Unfortunately for you, this means that she is driven to experiment to find out exactly how you differ. It is enthralling to see how you get angry, upset, enraged or whatever when she picks up that favourite ornament and tries to shove it through the cat flap. Her motivation here is not to deliberately annoy you, even if it seems that way, but really to find out how you work. She is as fascinated by that as she is interested in discovering why the lights go on and off when she presses the button, or why water comes out of the tap. It's all equally entertaining.

Focus on the important stuff

If you want to keep your sanity with a toddler, the first thing to do is to decide what is really important, and what can be ignored for the time being. It's not good for your state of mind or for your toddler's development to be continually saying 'no!' Children who constantly experience negative reactions from adults do not develop as well as others.

If you imagine that what is driving her at the moment is the need to know 'what will happen if I do this?' then it might help you see the world through her eyes a little more, and perhaps you can try to redirect that question into something not so destructive when needs be. If she is desperate to play with the taps, direct her to the outside tap or the cold tap in the utility room rather than the hot tap in the bathroom where she is in danger of scalding herself and flooding the house. If she likes pulling books out of the bookcase, put her own books on the accessible shelves and put your precious ones higher up. Believe it or not, she does still want to please you so redirection is always better than negativity.

Providing a safe environment

She can understand the word 'no', but has a poor memory, so you will find yourself saying it repeatedly. Be careful that the word does not lose its impact. It is better to decide beforehand what is really worth saying no about. Move precious objects out of sight; resign yourself to letting everything else be fiddled with.

Remember too that your toddler has no concept of danger and is depending on you to look out for her. Even if you try, for example, showing her how hot fire is, there is no guarantee that she will remember your lesson the next time she encounters flames. You need to rearrange your house with safety in mind. Lock away all hazards or put them well out of reach.

A playpen is fine for a crawling toddler, but once she can walk, it becomes too restrictive. Use the playpen in other, more creative ways – erect your Christmas tree or ironing board in it, or sit in it drinking a hot coffee without the risk of being scalded.

Setting boundaries

Once you have decided what behaviour has to be 'no', and what you will comfortably ignore for the time being, then you need to stick to your guns and have some sanctions for behaviour that is not acceptable. This is what setting boundaries means. All children are happier knowing what they can and cannot do, and will feel secure if these boundaries are set, and you will find out more about why this is in Chapter 06. Shifting boundaries – things that are 'no' today, and 'yes' tomorrow – confuse and worry your toddler, and in fact will make matters far worse for you in the long run. If you give in sometimes, and say yes today when yesterday it was no, she will try and try and try again so she can establish for herself when the answer is yes and when it is no. If she discovers that the answer will be yes if she screams loud enough, then guess what? She will scream until she gets her way and everyone loses out. She is not being naughty really; she has simply learnt that if she screams long enough and loud enough she will be allowed to have whatever she wants.

Reinforcing boundaries – disciplining your toddler

The term 'discipline' has a negative connotation these days, but the word actually has the same origin as disciple, and means, 'a training designed to engender self-control and an ordered way of life', or 'the state of self-control achieved by such training'. This is what you want, a toddler who has self-control. It's not going to happen overnight, but setting boundaries and sticking to these will help your child to gain self-control. Just as you should not 'sweat the small stuff', i.e. get worked up about things that don't really matter, your toddler will learn not to bother trying some things because they are a no go.

When your toddler is doing something you don't want her to do, part of the reward she gets from this is experiencing your reaction (even if this is incredibly negative, it is still exciting and stimulating). So the main punishment needs to be loss of stimulation and loss of interaction with you. This is why the naughty step works; putting your toddler somewhere away from you and making her sit still means loss of stimulation and lack of company.

The naughty step or naughty corner is the last resort, and you can warn your toddler that she is approaching the ultimate sanction. An ideal way to do this is to count her out, 'that's one...' and if she continues to misbehave she gets, 'that's two...' and finally, 'that's three...' at which point she is taken and put on the naughty step. The important point about the counting out is that it always stops at three with the naughty step. You don't want to get into counting up to ten or whatever, because then it will become interesting to find out just how high the numbers go, and which misdemeanour gets more numbers, and we are back to the experimenting toddler again.

Make sure you are explicit about what she has done wrong, and only criticize her behaviour – don't make comments about her as a person. For example, it is better to say, 'Throwing those bricks across the room was a very naughty thing to do! I am very cross about that!' rather than saying 'You naughty girl! You are very bad!'

Being an authoritative parent

People often get confused about the level of authority needed in parenting. We don't want to return to Victorian-style punishments, 'spare the rod and spoil the child', where thrashing was seen as the best way to get the message through. However, we still hear people saying, 'you'll spoil that baby if you pick it up all the time', and so there is a lingering feeling that too much responsiveness is not a good thing either.

Certainly for babies, there is no need to worry about channelling behaviour as babies are not capable of being manipulative or devious, and do not need boundaries, but when they become toddlers and start to become aware of their ability to affect the people around them, this is the time to impose boundaries for safety and also to start helping them to fit into our society.

At this point the need for some authority is important; but how to behave? There are four possibilities, broadly speaking, depending on whether you are asking a lot of your children or being fairly laid back, and whether you are willing to respond to them or unwilling to negotiate.

	Responsive	Unresponsive
Demanding	Authoritative	Authoritarian
Undemanding	Permissive	Uninvolved

The research evidence tends to indicate that authoritative parenting, where you set boundaries but are willing to explain these and negotiate, works best. Children whose parents are authoritative do well at school academically speaking, and are popular and sociable. Children whose parents are authoritarian tend to be less popular, isolated at school, and do less well academically, perhaps because having overly critical parents leads to loss of confidence.

Physical punishment

It is hard to measure the effects of physical punishment on children though studies have attempted to do so, quite apart from the moral implications. Longitudinal studies suggest that smacking does no harm within certain parameters, namely that it is under control, not in moments of anger, limited to young children and used in conjunction with reasoning. However, these boundaries are probably not ones in which smacking takes place – smacking is often something that is done in anger, and can easily escalate into physical abuse, and there is a lot of evidence that this is harmful to children.

There is a link in that children who misbehave or are aggressive also tend to be recipients of harsh physical punishment, though it is not clear that there is cause and effect here. But probably it is best to conclude that physical punishment may have harmful side effects, does not appear to have any benefits, and anyway, you are bigger and wiser than your child; surely you can find better ways of maintaining control?

Reinforcing good behaviour

We've looked at how to try to limit unwanted behaviour, but hand in hand with setting boundaries and imposing discipline must go reinforcing good behaviour. A child who only experiences negativity will lose self-confidence and stop trying to progress. So it is even more important that your toddler experiences praise and rewards for doing well. As a parent of a toddler you will need to make a conscious effort to do this; most of us are so relieved when our children behaves well that we relax, only focusing when they are misbehaving, but we then miss the opportunities to praise good behaviour. Also, if you are of British descent you were probably not raised with lots of praise and overt affection; the early twentieth century was very much about stiff upper lip and not showing emotions so, for many of us, our parents were not very demonstrative emotionally. Thus we need to make a conscious effort to be positive ourselves if we did not experience this type of parenting.

For example, when your toddler does something well, tell her that you are pleased. It is important to be explicit; general effusing is not really helpful: 'Thank you for being so helpful and for putting your toys away. I am really pleased.'

Case history: Alison and Alexander

For Alison, supermarkets have become almost a no-go zone. She's tried everything, but Alexander always ends up throwing an enormous tantrum. He either wants to get out of his seat, or if she lets him out he runs riot, and then he wants to fill the basket with all sorts of junk, and finally demands sweets until she either gives in or has him purple with rage.

Answer: Most children misbehave in supermarkets because they are tired, bored or hungry, so choose the right time to go; don't shop at the end of the day or with empty tummies, and make the trip entertaining. Alison could involve Alexander in writing the shopping list, and then letting him hunt for certain items. She needs to make it clear beforehand that she is not going to buy anything that is not on the list, but if he behaves he can have a pre-agreed reward, such as choosing a cake for tea.

The first few times may well be tricky, and Alison may have to be prepared for screams and yells or even abandoned shopping trolleys, but a few times without getting the promised reward or anything else for that matter, may well motivate Alexander to behave.

Tantrums

There is no one answer to dealing with tantrums, possibly because each child is different and the reason they have tantrums is probably different. Some children have more tantrums than others, just as some adults are more likely to lose their tempers than others.

One point that is common to all children is that they only have tantrums when they are with close family, so tantrums are not just about losing your temper, but are in effect about feeling negative with the people you love. Some psychologists think that toddlers are in conflict; their desire to be independent battling with the desire to stay a baby, others claim that tantrums are about frustration. Yet another interesting perspective is that although the first tantrum is genuine, when your toddler is swept away by the force of her own rage, after this your toddler is aware of what she's doing and is actually in control, so these tantrums are about having an effect on adults.

Whatever the reason for the tantrums, there are several things that would make your life easier.

- Have clear boundaries and stick to them. Your toddler will be less likely to throw a tantrum about something when she knows she does not have a chance of winning. For instance, if your toddler is never given a sweet at the supermarket and knows this is a no-go issue, then she won't bother throwing a wobbly about it.
- Try to work out what the flashpoints are for your toddler's tantrum, and pre-empt them. Look out for signs of trouble brewing and try to head it off. For instance, does she lose it when she is hungry or tired? Bringing meal times forward or having mid-meal snacks may help.
- Work out a strategy when everything is calm; it actually doesn't matter as long as it works for you, but make sure your toddler realizes that tantrums don't achieve anything. So no rewards, no giving in.

    Strategies can be a distraction – walking away, telling her off, ignoring her, yelling back or hugging her – it's up to you. But don't ever let her have what she wants because she is throwing a tantrum, and when she has calmed down, explain that this behaviour is not acceptable. If she consistently tantrums then you will have to punish her too – make her go to her room or sit on the naughty step; whatever will make her understand that this behaviour is not acceptable and has consequences.
- Think too about your own response. Often your toddler will tantrum when you can least cope; the end of the day when you are tired, or when you are out in a public place. If your toddler is canny enough to push your buttons at the right time, you too can rise above this and head the confrontation off, with some foresight and planning!

Summary of this chapter

- Toddlers are in conflict – being mobile is dangerous, but they are also driven to explore. Perhaps one of the reasons they so easily lose it, is that they cannot cope with being thwarted with no obvious reason.
- Your toddler has only just discovered that you have a separate existence from her, and she finds it incredibly interesting to experiment and see what really pushes your buttons.

- You need to decide what is important and what is not – try not to say 'no' too often.
- You must set boundaries and stick to them, with consequences for misbehaviour.
- It is equally important to reward good behaviour.
- Tantrums can occur for many reasons, and discovering what they are about will help you to stop them. However, your toddler must be made to understand that they are not an acceptable way to behave.

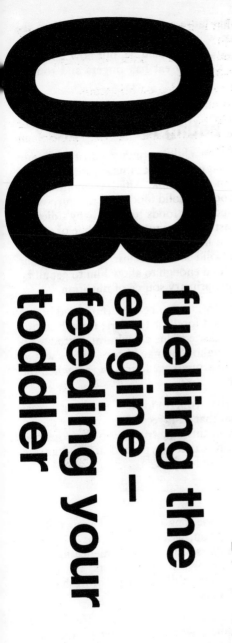

03

fuelling the engine – feeding your toddler

In this chapter you will learn:
- why toddlers become faddy about foods
- why fat-rich foods and sugar are so tempting
- how to establish good eating habits early in life
- how to eliminate junk food from your toddler's diet.

There is probably no topic more emotive for parents than the foods our children will or will not eat. We probably all have a good idea of what healthy eating should be, but how does that help when your toddler will only eat fish fingers and tomato ketchup?

What is healthy eating for a toddler?

For the first year of life, your child's primary nutrition would have come from milk, be that breast milk or its substitute – baby formula milk derived from cow's milk. After six months, you would have gradually introduced solid foods, but the purpose of this was mainly to introduce new foods to your baby's diet, to let him experiment with tastes and textures, and while of course that food should have been healthy, it could never fulfil all his nutritional needs because solid foods are just too bulky; your baby's stomach could not hold enough to allow him to get all he needed. Milk was and is his primary source of nutrition.

So even for toddlers, milk continues to be important, and breast milk is still an ideal, all-round food for toddlers, though in our society, few toddlers are breastfed, due to cultural attitudes. In most of the world, and throughout human history, babies would have been breastfed up until around age four to seven, when the milk teeth start to fall out.

Given that it is unlikely that your toddler is receiving breast milk, it is even more crucial that he is receiving a healthy diet in other ways. Unfortunately in this country, due to the power of the food industry, the options that are pushed at children are often the least healthy possible foods.

The ideal diet

What you are aiming for in the long term is that your toddler will eat the same foods as you, assuming you eat a healthy balanced diet. If you currently subsist on convenience foods, it might be a good time to change your eating habits, as we shall see. Ideally you would feed your toddler a variety of fresh foods, avoiding added sugars and salts.

Carbohydrates, found in bread, pasta and cereals, are essential energy foods for your toddler. Wholegrain cereals have more essential nutrients as they have undergone less processing.

Protein comes from lean meat, fish, eggs, dairy products such as cheese or yoghurt, beans and lentils. Protein builds bones and muscles, and we all need some protein in our diets, but many of us eat too much. If you eat low fat products, remember that your child needs higher proportions of healthy fats.

Fruit and vegetables are an essential part of the diet. Raw fruit and vegetables are particularly healthy, and steaming or microwaving preserves more vitamins than boiling. Dried and fresh fruits can be given as healthy, between-meal snacks.

The issues

All sounds simple, doesn't it? But food can become such an issue with toddlers, with mealtimes stressing everyone out. So let's consider what the issues are and why they happen in the first place.

Issue 1 – the three meals a day myth

The first battle often comes about because parents mistakenly think that their toddlers must have three meals a day. Where has this come from? If we think about what we evolved to eat, we were primarily grazers, foraging for food, eating when we found things – little and often. We were, for most of our history, hunters and gatherers, and probably as such did not sit down for three meals a day. Fairly recently in human history, we became farmers and started cultivating our foods, but we don't know whether we then started having three meals a day or not, perhaps we continued to graze, simply eating more cereals.

In fact, even the Victorians had at least four meals a day (at least those who could afford it did) – breakfast, lunch, tea, supper, not forgetting elevenses etc. And if you keep a log of what you eat and drink in 24 hours, you will probably find that you consume something every couple of hours; a cup of tea or coffee, a drink of water, snacks, etc. The three meals a day habit is not particularly natural. It's far better to eat when you are hungry and to spread your food throughout the day; this way you avoid over-eating and also keep your blood sugar levels stable.

Children's stomachs are much smaller than ours, and eating little and often is a reasonable strategy. If you try to make them go too long between meals, they are likely to become either crabby and irritable or hyperactive, as their blood sugar goes up and down. Also the first step in preventing obesity is to allow children to regulate their own appetites. Babies are born with the ability to detect when they have had enough to eat; that is why supply and demand breastfeeding works and why breastfed babies are not usually overweight. One reason children become overweight is because parents override their satiation cues, forcing them to finish the bottle or, later on, clear their plates.

Parents often complain that their toddlers won't sit still for meals, but want to rush off and play again – that they want to graze all day rather than sit down and eat. In fact that is probably what nature intended they do. It is only a recent cultural idea that we should sit down and eat a large meal at a set time.

Nevertheless, mealtimes are sometimes the only occasion when a family will sit down together and communicate, so it is not a bad habit to get into. Eating together builds social bonds, and is an important part of the fabric of daily life. However, instead of thinking of mealtimes as being about cramming as much food into your toddler as possible, think of it as a sit down, social occasion, with food as the secondary consideration. Accept that your toddler may not eat much, and may well want food again a couple of hours later. Instead of planning for three large meals a day; think of offering main meals, but also plan for healthy snacks between meals, like cheese cubes, sandwiches or fruit slices. What you need to avoid is your child eating junk snacks between meals, like crisps or biscuits, as these will then become more attractive than the main meals, as we shall see below, and you will be battling to get your child to attempt to eat anything at all at main mealtime.

The other reason for allowing your toddler to decide how much to eat and whether to eat at all is that early experiences set up physiological expectations in our body, and in the case of food, this may be expectations about how much food your body needs to operate. Allowing your child to regulate their own appetite, while controlling sugar and fat surges, will set up the right regulatory habits.

Healthy snacks for the hungry toddler

- Cream cheese sandwich on whole grain bread.
- Bananas, apples, raw carrots, sticks of celery, dried fruit.
- Scrambled eggs, tuna or sardines on toast.
- Slices or cubes of cheese.
- Dried and fresh fruit cut into smaller portions, e.g. apple boats, half grapes, raisins.

Issue 2 – worrying about weight

Closely linked to the worry about whether or not your toddler will sit down to eat a meal, is the worry about his weight. Is he overweight, underweight, just right, and does it matter?

The 'ideal' weight for children or adults has always been governed by fashion. Throughout history, and in other societies today where food is scarce, being plump or even fat is considered healthy. In our society now, where food is abundant, thin is seen as best, certainly for adults, and there is a growing trend away from seeing chubby children or babies as healthy. If you look at old baby books, from the 1960s say, you will see pictures of very plump babies being viewed as somehow 'ideal' whereas baby magazines today tend to show leaner babies, ones which would have been considered unhealthily skinny a couple of generations ago.

No one can say for sure what is ideal for babies, but your toddler's personal health record contains two centile charts, which plot his weight and height from one to five years of age. These are based on the average of you and your partner's height, the idea being that your child should gain weight and stature very roughly as expected from his genetic inheritance. (So if either you or your partner is out of the normal range, or if your baby was very premature, the charts may not be accurate, and of course these are really just a guestimate.) If you are worried that your toddler doesn't appear to eat enough, the charts may be reassuring – if you can see that he is gaining in both height and weight as the charts predict, then you may feel more relaxed. But of course they can be a double-edged sword if your toddler is not growing as predicted!

If you are at all concerned about your toddler's weight, then talk to your health visitor and your GP; they can assess your child's development accurately and objectively, and give you particular advice about diet and exercise if needs be.

Rather than worry about your toddler's weight, it is better to concentrate on providing healthy foods at regular intervals. Think of yourself as responsible for **what, when** and **where**, and let your toddler be responsible for **how much** and **whether**. So your job is to provide regular healthy meals, and encourage him to be aware of his own feelings of hunger and satiation by letting him respond to these by neither over-eating nor starving. Don't attempt to control whether your child will eat what you provide and how much he will eat. Believe it or not, left to their own devices, children would actually eat a naturally balanced diet. They may only eat fruit one day, protein the next, and then gorge on carbohydrates for a few days, but if you average it all out, they are pretty good at controlling their intake, if they are given healthy options in the first place.

If your family could do with losing a few pounds, it is important to increase your levels of activity as being more active will increase your metabolism which in turn will burn up more calories. Simply cutting down on the calories may not work on its own, as the body responds to this by decreasing the amount of energy it burns. Of course, you should also cut out any unhealthy aspects of your diet, such as too much sugar and saturated fat. Try to eat healthy foods, little and often, so that you never feel hungry. This also keeps your blood sugar stable and will stop any temptation to binge.

Eating disorders

Children are becoming obsessed about being thin at a younger and younger age. If you diet or worry about your weight, it is really important that you don't make negative comments in front of your children. You are their role model, if you avoid eating or talk about not getting fat, your children will copy you – perhaps with disastrous results.

Issue 3 – faddy eaters

Many toddlers seem to want to subsist on a tiny range of foods, and this is worrying. It may be helpful to understand where this comes from in the first place.

The first tastes babies have is usually breast milk, which is incredibly sweet – far sweeter than cow's milk. After that, babies are often weaned onto pureed vegetables and fruit (like carrots, apples, pears and bananas) and these too are fairly sweet. So, inevitably, your baby has a sweet tooth to begin with. However, he was also getting used to your own diet in the womb and in the early months, firstly in the amniotic fluid, and later the breast milk, would taste of whatever you were eating. Babies being weaned onto solids accept new tastes far more readily if they have experienced them already in the womb or through breastfeeding.

On the whole, younger babies are more open to new tastes anyway, and parents can feel quite smug when comparing notes at this stage, 'oh he adores spinach' 'my baby likes moussaka' etc. However, toddlers often shut right down and refuse everything – new tastes, even tastes they have accepted before. One reason may be to do with some ancient survival mechanism. Once he becomes mobile he is in danger of picking up and eating something poisonous when the person in charge of him lets their attention stray. So perhaps he restricts what he will eat down to familiar tastes, particularly those which are sweet, rejecting bitter as this is often synonymous with poisonous foods. Once this happens, perhaps he will only start accepting new and strange tastes when he is able to tell himself logically that 'this food is probably ok, and let's ignore the fact that it tastes strange and go with it, because apparently it is quite nice'. For the amenable child this might happen early on, for the less amenable child it might not happen until they are old enough to buy it themselves...

So the moral is, introduce as many tastes when weaning as possible, and serve them up regularly so he doesn't forget them, but you may still have to accept a narrowing down of tastes at some point. Accept that all children dislike certain foods, but don't worry – there are always alternatives. If what you're offering is generally healthy and balanced, even food fads will be no problem. If your toddler senses that you are anxious that he 'should' eat a particular food, he may refuse it as a way of asserting independence. You need to concentrate on offering varied meals that are generally healthy and balanced, and try to be relaxed about how much he eats or whether he eats at all.

Encourage him to regard food as something to be explored and enjoyed. Finger foods will help him gain fine finger control as well as giving him independence. If he is a fussy eater, he may well relish the chance to feed himself.

Ways to tackle food fads

Food will be more appealing if you:

1 don't serve too much at once
2 separate the ingredients out so they can see what they're eating
3 keep it crunchy. Soggy vegetables are unappealing and in fact less healthy
4 avoid giving sweets or other unhealthy foods as treats or rewards; use toys or comics instead
5 praise them when they eat well; ignore it when they fuss.

Food as treats

While we want to avoid food being a source of conflict, we should also try to avoid it becoming associated with comfort. Try to avoid using food as a treat or reward too often. When you want to reward your toddler for doing something well, aim to have a variety of little treats on hand. These could be colouring books, an extra story at bedtime, a small outing, an extra episode of his favourite video – you can be quite creative here. The point is to avoid giving sweets or biscuits every time (occasionally is fine).

If every reward, every treat, is something to eat, then your toddler may well grow up to associate food with emotional sustenance, and if he feels low later in life, he may then over-eat to comfort himself.

Healthy party foods

Parties are often the time when all good intentions go out of the window. Here are some suggestions for healthy alternatives to crisps and chicken nuggets:

- **Crudités and dips:** Arrange a tempting array of raw vegetables around some dips. Red and yellow peppers, carrot batons, celery sticks, cherry tomatoes. For dips, try plain cottage cheese, cream cheese or fromage frais, or flavour with avocado and lemon or pineapple juice.
- **Sandwich selection:** An easy and satisfying finger food. Use unsalted butter on wholemeal bread and a selection of fillings like mashed banana, jam or cheese.

- **Popcorn**: Put a layer of sunflower oil at the bottom of a pan and add one layer of unpopped corn kernels. Put the lid on the pan and heat. After a couple of minutes you will hear the corn popping. When the popping slows down, take it off the heat. You can flavour with a sprinkling of salt or sugar.
- **Fruit platter or fruit kebabs**: Arrange a variety of fruit chopped into bite size pieces on a large platter, or thread onto sticks. Try kiwi fruit, cherries, strawberries, red and green grapes, tangerine segments and pineapple chunks.
- **Milk shake/fruit smoothies**: In a liquidizer, blend fruit with milk and/or yogurt and if possible, crushed ice. Try bananas, strawberries, coconut, peaches.

Issue 4 – fat and sugar cravings

Why do we have such issues with fat and sugar? The problem is that human beings' access to food has changed dramatically in the last century; our ancestors spent most of their waking hours foraging for something to eat, initially subsisting on roots, berries and leaves with the occasional protein feast when they managed to catch something more substantial. The reason we now crave fat and sugar is that these are calorific foods, but were generally not that easy to come by, so the more powerful our ancestors' craving for these foods, the more effort they would put into finding them. Successful foragers survived and passed this craving on to us.

Our ancestors' sweet tooth had to be satisfied with fruit, far healthier than the refined sugar we eat today. They feasted on wild animals or fish when they could; however both of these have a much lower fat content than our domesticated cattle (about 4 per cent in wild meat compared to 25–30 per cent in domesticated animals) and to make matters worse, the fat of wild game is about five times higher in polyunsaturated fats whereas modern cattle contain the more dangerous saturated fats. Domestication of cattle has also provided us with a cheap source of fat-rich dairy products like milk, cream and cheese, which again if eaten to excess contain too much in the way of saturated fats.

Refined, processed foods are cheap, have a long shelf-life and with added artificial flavourings, enhanced fat and sugar, they are also tempting to eat. The evidence is now overwhelming that highly processed food leads to health problems such as heart disease, diabetes and obesity. Processing inevitably destroys much of the goodness; vitamins are killed off by high heat for instance, and have to be added back into foods, and added vitamins are not absorbed as well as the naturally occurring ones. Colourings and preservatives cause behavioural problems such as ADHD in susceptible children. Even if your child is not overweight, feeding him the wrong types of fat clogs up his insides, creating health problems later in life.

Case history: Arleen and Charlotte

'I found that Charlotte will not eat a huge plateful of food mixed together, but if I put out a platter with lots of different things she will happily help herself to most of it. So instead of doing a stew, I offer meat, vegetables and sauce separately and she takes some of everything. Instead of fruit salad I do a fruit platter; I arrange all the fruit pieces on a large plate and let her select what she wants. I have also found that she is more willing to eat something if she was involved in preparing it. If she helps me scrub potatoes, stir sauces and generally gets involved throughout, she is far more willing to eat the end product. Finally I have also discovered a great snack for out and about which she absolutely adores: an avocado. I chop it in half and give her slices – seems to me a really healthy snack.'

Dump the junk

No one expects that busy parents should have to home-cook everything, but equally it is not sensible to rely totally on convenience foods. Buy food as close to its raw state as possible. This does not mean spending hours preparing everything; grilled chicken breast and salad takes the same amount of time to prepare as a microwave dinner for instance. It's also important to aim for variety in your shopping trolley.

Alternative junk foods

If your child is already addicted to junk food, here are some suggestions as to how to wean him off this gradually onto healthier options:

Food type	What's wrong with it	Making it healthier	The home-made, ultra healthy, alternative!
Fizzy drinks: lemonade, coke, etc.	No nutrition at all, high in sugar and lots of additives.	Look for drinks containing just fruit juice, sugar and fizz.	Wean your child onto fizzy water flavoured with fruit slices.
Squash	No nutrition at all, high in sugar and lots of additives.	Dilute pure fruit juice with water.	Add slices of fruit and mint leaves to tap water.
Fruit juice drinks	Very high in sugar – minimal fruit.	Wean onto pure fruit juices.	Make your own freshly squeezed fruit juice or smoothie!
Savoury snacks – crisps, Skips, Wotsits etc.	Very high in salt and the wrong kinds of fat, particularly the shaped versions.	Choose the plainest crisps and read the label – the fewer ingredients the better.	Oatcakes, rice cakes and breadsticks are healthier snacks, or make your own popcorn.
Cheese strings/ processed cheese/ lunchables	Very little nutrition, highly processed and one portion exceeds a child's RDA salt.	The pick and mix cheeses do contain some real cheeses.	Better still, and less expensive, cut cheddar into cubes and serve with cubes of pineapple.

Chips	Can be high in salt and very unhealthy if deep-fried in old oil.	Choose large, oven baked chips brushed with fresh sunflower oil.	Cut whole raw potatoes into wedges, brush with olive oil, and roast at high temperature for 20 mins. Cut root vegetables like parsnip or carrot into chip shapes and roast.
Burgers	High in the wrong types of fat and salt.	Choose those made with lean, high quality meat and grill or dry fry them.	Home-made is easy and a better bet as you will use higher-grade mince.
Chicken/ turkey nuggets and shapes	Anything coated with breadcrumbs will absorb more fat. Usually lowest grade meat.	Make your own – dip chicken breast in egg and bread-crumbs then grill.	Grilled chicken breast or drumsticks are the healthiest option.
Pizza	Dough usually made from highly processed flour and unhealthy fats; many toppings also unhealthy.	Go for vegetable topped or plain cheese. Avoid processed cheese and salty meats like pepperoni.	Try ciabatta bread grilled with cheese and vegetable toppings.
Sausage rolls and meat pies	High in salt, unhealthy fats, cheap meat. Pastry often has flour bleached with chlorine.	Cheese straws are a healthier pastry snack.	Try baked potatoes with fillings such as cheese, mince or tuna.

Children's yoghurts and fromage frais	They look appealing but are full of sugar.	Adult yoghurts tend to have less sugar.	Buy full cream yoghurt and add your own fruit or fruit puree.
Hot dogs and sausages	Hot dogs and the cheaper sausages, especially those targeted at children, have poor quality meat, additives, and too much salt.	With sausages the more you spend the better. Cut large butcher sausages into child size portions and grill.	Try brown pitta bread with melted cheese and salad garnish as an alternative to hot dog in a roll.
White bread	So much goodness and taste is taken out of the flour in white bread that manufacturers have to enhance the flavours artificially!	If your child refuses brown bread, try mighty white or best of both – white bread with some bran.	The best bread is wholemeal so try to wean your child onto it, perhaps disguising it as toast or using fillings like mashed banana.
Sweets	No nutrition, heaps of chemicals and too much sugar.	Dark chocolate contains iron, calcium and zinc.	Use dried fruit or try fresh fruit dipped in melted chocolate.
Tinned spaghetti/ children's pasta shapes	Along the right lines, but too much sugar and salt.	Many shops sell dried pasta for children in animal shapes.	The best pasta is wholemeal – and it has more taste too!

Ice lollies/ ice cream	Many lollies have no nutrition, heaps of chemicals and too much sugar.	Pure fruit ice lollies are fine, although they often have too much sugar.	Good quality ice cream is healthier, especially if topped with a sauce of fruit puree.
Jelly	Mostly a big no-no – chemicals and sugar – that's it!	Healthier versions available in health food shops. Stir in whole fruit pieces before setting.	Even better – a fruit salad with double cream or Greek yoghurt. Mix in honey or crushed sesame seed bars.
Children's cereals – frosted or chocolate coated	Again, why is the unhealthiest option targeted at children? Not a good way to start the day.	Rice Krispies and Cornflakes are healthier cereals, although they still contain too much sugar and practically no fibre.	Go for Shredded Wheat, Puffed Wheat, Raisin Wheats, Weetabix – just pure wheat if possible. Try home-made porridge for winter mornings or muesli – rolled oats with fresh fruit and yogurt for a yummy start to the day!

Baked beans	These have fibre, protein and vitamins – not bad – but also a lot of sugar and salt – 2g in the average helping.	Versions from the wholefood shop have less sugar.	You can make your own – haricot beans in tomato sause – that's all it is!
Cakes	Shop bought are high in sugar and salt, additives and may have peanuts as well as chemicals like bleach.	Look out for healthy versions like carrot cake or gingerbread, or offer scones, muffins or croissants.	Home-made cakes – fun to make with your kids and satisfying treats in the winter months.
Dried packet dessert mixes	Look yummy but there is nothing in them of nutritional value.	Tinned rice pudding or semolina with jam are good alternatives.	Better still – home-made trifle.
Biscuits	As with cakes, high in sugar and salt, additives and may have peanuts.	Digestive biscuits or hob nobs are not too bad. Breadsticks and rice cakes are excellent.	Try shortbread or flapjack as easy to make at home options.

Baffled by bread?

Ever wondered which brown bread is best?

- Wholemeal bread is made with 100 per cent whole-grain flour, so it undergoes the least processing, and should therefore contain the most vitamins and minerals, as well as the most fibre.
- Brown bread is made with 50 per cent whole-grain flour. Lacking wheat germ, it is lower on vitamins and fibre.

- Granary is a trade name for wheatmeal (not wholemeal) flour to which malted wheat grains are added.

- High-fibre white bread is made from refined flour with pea-plant fibre added; again it lacks the nutritional value of wholemeal bread.

Summary of this chapter

- Toddlers naturally restrict the variety of food they will accept, but you can work around this.
- Your role is to control what, when and where, and let your toddler be responsible for how much and whether.
- Fat and sugar are meant to be tempting, and food manufacturers use this to their advantage.
- Make mealtimes social times and ignore how much food is actually being consumed.
- It is hard to say what an ideal weight is, but if your toddler is eating a variety of healthy foods he is unlikely to be overweight. If he does need to lose weight, increase his activity levels rather than cutting down his food.
- Convenience foods are a life-saver when you are just too busy to prepare something else; don't worry about the odd pizza or hot dog. Just avoid it becoming the main part of your children's diet.
- Above all though, try to stay relaxed about food. As long as you generally aim to provide a varied diet your toddler will thrive.

04

toilet time

In this chapter you will learn:
- when your toddler is likely to be ready for toilet training
- how to toilet train your toddler
- what to do about toilet talk and masturbation.

Being toilet trained is another stepping stone on your toddler's path to independence. In this chapter we will look at the physical and emotional developments that enable your baby to be clean and dry, as well as the inevitable consequence of that extra freedom – masturbation and toilet talk.

Fashions in toilet training

As you're probably already discovering, parenting methods change with each generation, and toilet training is yet another area where everyone has an opinion.

In some cultures, nappies are unheard of; instead mothers become adept at predicting when babies are going to perform so they can hold them over the nearest bush! This 'natural' training is now becoming popular in the West, but whether this is a fad or something that is actually going to catch on, we will have to wait and see. The idea with this method is that you become so attuned to your baby's signals; you can see something happening before it happens and you then catch it on a potty. However, given that nappies are fairly convenient, whether you are using washable or disposables, it hardly seems worth the bother. Being able to predict a motion and catch it on a pot may save you some cleaning up, but it won't mean your child is toilet trained any more quickly.

Before disposable nappies and washing machines, women were understandably keen to avoid too much washing and our grandmothers would 'pot' from birth. They achieved their early successes by creating a 'conditioned reflex', teaching babies to associate the cold rim of a potty with performing, particularly after feeding when they would probably go anyway. This worked because babies had a strict, regular feeding routine, but it wasn't 'toilet training' in that the babies were not consciously able to control their bladder or bowels.

You may feel under pressure from Granny or perhaps from your peers to get your baby out of nappies, particularly if your baby's contemporaries are using potties already. However, there is little point in trying to toilet train before your child is physically or emotionally ready.

How bowel and bladder control develop

Once feeding is established, a newborn baby will wee up to 20 times a day, completely involuntarily. Bowel movements are less frequent, but also outside your baby's control. With time, your baby wees less frequently; you may notice her nappy stays dry for longer. Some babies dislike being wet or dirty, others don't seem to care, but whatever your baby feels about this sensation, it doesn't mean that she's also aware of passing the substance which makes her uncomfy. Eventually she will become aware of the sensation of passing urine or faeces; pausing as if wondering what is happening; but even then she's still not quite capable of being toilet trained.

The crucial stage is when your baby becomes aware of the sensation of needing to go before actually doing so, usually any time after 18 months, and once this happens, she can start to 'hang on' by deliberate control, although at first for no more than a few seconds. This is really the earliest time at which potty training may have some success – usually with bowel control first.

How will I know when my toddler is ready?

Apart from achieving these physical milestones, your child also needs to be emotionally ready. Toilet training involves gradually acquiring a huge range of skills – becoming aware of a need, communicating this need, holding on until a toilet is found, managing doors, clothing, toilet paper, flushing toilets and washing hands.

- Is your toddler capable of understanding and accepting the idea of using a toilet or potty?
- Will you be able to explain what is needed, and will she be able to tell you when she needs to go?
- In general, is she striving to be independent, or is she still clinging on to her babyhood?

Toilet training is about growing up and growing away from you, and not all children want this at the same age. On the other hand, how amenable and co-operative is your toddler right now? If she is generally being negative about life, getting to the pot on time will be another thing for you to battle about.

Getting started

You have two main options with toilet training, which boil down to being child-led or adult-led. Child-led means waiting until your child expresses an interest in toilet training herself. This is unlikely to happen until your child is well past her second birthday, but the advantage of waiting this long is that you will probably have relatively few accidents. A less stressful method, it's likely to work as your child is demonstrating her own desire for independence, and is probably aware of her capabilities. If you are likely to react badly to frequent accidents, then this is the method for you.

If you can't wait for your child to show willing, perhaps because a nursery place is dependent on some progress away from nappies, you can, of course, decide yourself that 'this is the time'. The first step is to find out how often your baby needs to wee, perhaps watching her around bath time or in the garden. If she can't go for more than two hours, you will have a lot of running around.

Involve your toddler in the decision to start. Let her shop with you for a potty and knickers. You will probably want to have potties in different places. You can start gradually, encouraging her to sit on the pot at certain times of the day – after meals for instance, or when you go to the toilet. At first she may not stay on for more than a few seconds, but this is fine. In time you can perhaps extend the period by watching TV together or reading a book. Reward and encourage any successes or near attempts, but don't be over the top and certainly don't scold messes.

You could just decide, 'Today's the day' and abandon nappies all together. This all or nothing approach can work with an older toddler, but you will need to stay at home for a few days and be ready to cope in a laid back way with frequent accidents. Roll up carpets, and get a supply of old clothes ready. Try to avoid stressful or busy periods, such as moving house, Christmas, or when a new baby is imminent. This all or nothing method works better in warmer weather, when your toddler can wander about with a bare bottom.

In general, praise and encouragement are fine, but don't overdo it. If you have to coerce your toddler, she is not ready. If she senses that this is a big issue for you, then you are giving her a wonderful tool to control you with. Accidents will happen, and go on for some time. Generally speaking, girls are quicker than boys, bowel control comes before bladder and daytime dryness before night, but with all these stages, your child will get there eventually. If you are having little success, then don't be afraid to stop – she may just not be ready yet.

Toilet training tips

- Travel pots, which have small sealable inner bags, can help when out and about at first.
- Most children find toilets hard to use for quite some time, as they are too high and the bowl is too big. Potties are better as they encourage children to squat, which is the natural position for letting go.
- Decide on your terminology beforehand, and be sure that you are happy for your child to use it at the top of her voice in all circumstances. Most adults, including teachers, nursery staff and doctors are used to 'wee and poo'.
- Using pull-ups instead of nappies does not usually work as toddlers just treat these like normal nappies. Pull ups can help when you are going out and can't afford to have an accident, but it is better to just take spare clothes with you at all times.

Case history: Jess and Andrea

Andrea seemed to be progressing ok with toilet training, but now she has started to hang on to poos and will only do these if she has a nappy on. Jess has tried everything, but Andrea just gets more and more distressed, hanging on in desperation until she puts her nappy back on. It is obvious that she knows when she is going to go, but won't do it in the right place.

Answer: this is far more common than you might think. Children often regress in bowel control if they have had a scare. Perhaps they got a bit constipated on one occasion and passing the motion hurt. It is worth Jess visiting her GP just to check if Andrea is constipated.

Sometimes the fear is about the toilet itself; perhaps Andrea is afraid she is going to fall into it, or perhaps the sound of the flush is frightening her. See if she can explain what the fears are about. Other children will regress for reasons that are nothing to do with the toilet training per se, but because they are under stress elsewhere – a new sibling is a common cause for instance, or a change at nursery.

The most important thing is not to push her. Let her regress for a while and try again later. Sometimes it is better to forget all about it for a few weeks, take the pressure off. Jess could start a star chart, where she gets a star if she does a poo in the toilet or potty, and once she has three stars, she gets a special treat. Don't take stars away for accidents, and don't comment on the mistakes, just remark on the successes.

Masturbation

It is around this time that your toddler will become fascinated by genitals – her own and other people's. Toilet training gives her access to her own in a way that was not possible before, and she may well be interested in exploring, though on the whole boys are far more interested. There are many possible reasons for this gender difference; boys' genitals are more visible and obvious, but also traditionally parents have been far more shocked when their daughter masturbates and girls pick up on this and desist. There is no reason to feel like this, so try not to over-react. Distraction is always the best way to stop it if it happens too frequently or in the wrong place.

Children are not born predisposed to see sex or masturbation as particularly special. It's no more interesting than electricity or puddles or any other fascinating topic. It's our culture which teaches children that sex has a snigger factor. You can't single-handedly make sex a neutral topic; what's important instead is to establish acceptable behaviour, and to ensure that home is a place where it's ok to ask questions.

Using appropriate language

With both boys and girls, use words you feel comfortable for your child to use. So don't use slang, but don't use anatomically correct words either. You don't want your child shouting about her vagina in the supermarket. Childhood euphemisms are fine – we talk about tummies not intestines; in the same way you can say bottom instead of anus, and willy instead of penis. You do need to decide on an acceptable name for girl's sexual organs.

Leaving them nameless suggests that girls have no sexual organs or that they're not important. Your daughter may find it difficult to come to terms with her own genitals if you do not give them a name (equivalent to 'willy') which you will find acceptable for her to use. 'Fanny' is an innocuous possibility. As you will see in Chapter 18, language acquisition is part of the development of thought in your child and it is easier for your toddler to hold a concept in her mind if she has a word for it.

Children love smutty talk. For them, it is about coming to terms with the meaning their bodies have in society. Smutty talk is understandable, but it needs to be kept in check. Establish rules and boundaries, for instance, bottom jokes are ok in your own bedroom but not at the table. Poo talk will upset Granny, but Mummy turns a blind eye to the occasional joke. Incidentally, a very useful phrase to use from now on is 'bottoms are private'. This is a rule which not only sets boundaries, but is also starting to put protection in place for your children.

Smutty talk from visiting children needs to be handled in the same way as you might handle other bad behaviour. 'We don't use that word here, Michael.' If your child comes home with a really offensive word or phrase, try to find out where they heard it and follow this up if necessary. Again be calm and set limits: 'That word is not nice, we don't use it.'

Summary of this chapter

- Toilet training methods come in and out of fashion, but your child is unlikely to be truly toilet trained until she is physically and emotionally ready.
- You can be child-led, adult-led, do it gradually or go for broke.
- Masturbation is a natural part of growing up – try not to let it become an issue.
- Toilet talk is inevitable at this stage; set sensible boundaries which are not too rigid.

05

sleep and your toddler

In this chapter you will learn:
- how much sleep your toddler needs
- about settling your toddler in the evenings
- why your toddler might be waking in the night and what to do about it.

It may seem, on the face of it, that if you are having a battle either putting your toddler to bed or keeping him there it probably means he now needs less sleep, but this is usually not true. Some children who don't get enough sleep will be grumpy, irritable and generally difficult, but other tired children become hyperactive; the more tired they are, the more manic and out of control they can seem. Either scenario sound familiar? If your child is generally cheerful and contented, alert and active, he may well be getting enough sleep, but if he's difficult during the day, then perhaps he's over-tired.

How much sleep does my toddler need?

Roughly speaking, at 18 months, your toddler still needs 12 hours of sleep a night and up to two hours during the day; by the age of three they will still need 12 hours at night but may have dropped the day-time sleep, although a quiet rest after lunch is good for recharging batteries. He should also be able to go through the night without your help. Having said that, many parents of toddlers have bedtime battles; if this applies to you then it's worth unpicking why your toddler is not sleeping enough, and this may help you to implement any necessary changes.

I won't go to bed! Getting your toddler settled in the evenings

As we saw in Chapter 02, toddlers need boundaries, and night-times are when they can really make an impact! Once your toddler realizes that you stay up and have fun in the evenings, he is going to be less keen to go to bed himself. Add to this feeling tired and out of sorts, and he's bound to be unreasonable. What he really needs is for you to be firm, to set boundaries calmly and with gentle persistence. Screaming at him to go to sleep will only work him up more.

Developing a happy bedtime routine

If you haven't yet established a bedtime routine, now's really the time. Winding down, with the same sequence of calming events each night, helps your toddler feel secure and dozy. It doesn't really matter what you choose to do; a bedtime routine is basically about keeping things predictable. A suggested routine could be as follows:

- bath
- milky drink
- brush teeth
- goodnight kiss downstairs for everyone
- bedtime story in bed
- kiss and cuddle, and both say 'night, night!'

Getting the temperature right

A drop in body temperature is one of the most important 'triggers' for sleep; normally your core body temperature drops just before you nod off; that's why it's hard to get to sleep if you're too hot. So to help your toddler doze off easily, let him have a hot bath before bed. This will raise his temperature briefly, and when he gets out and his temperature starts to drop, he should feel sleepy.

You will also need to make sure that his hands and feet are warm enough in bed, because if his extremities are colder than his core, he will not be able to nod off. If he does get cold hands and feet, a hot-water bottle at the foot of the cot before bedtime (taken out just before he gets into bed) may help.

So:

- make sure your toddler's hands and feet are not cold
- give him a hot bath at bedtime
- no large meals or running around just before bedtime either.

I don't want to be alone! Leaving your toddler to go to sleep

Many toddlers develop separation anxiety, and need extra reassurance before being left to settle down for the night. Watch out for this turning into a delaying tactic!

If you find that settling your toddler is taking longer and longer:

- follow your routine of story, kisses and cuddles, plus lots of reassurance
- decide on a time limit for settling your toddler, and stick to it firmly
- leave a night-light on or a lullaby tape playing after you leave.

Crying it out

Many books will suggest leaving your toddler to cry it out is best. The principle behind this so called 'controlled crying' is that your toddler has 'learned' that when he cries, you will respond, so not responding when he cries will teach him that it's not worth crying, and he will, after a few evenings of no response, just fall asleep.

Although people will say it does work, and indeed children who are left to cry do eventually stop crying, this is really focusing on a short-term gain without thinking about any long-term loss to you or your child. Research evidence does not back this up as a successful strategy when attempted on its own; it works best when done with the supervision and support of experienced professional helpers, such as sleep clinic workers.

Babies who know that their parents respond to their needs are more secure. Leaving your toddler to cry himself to sleep does go against this, though whether it will have much of an effect if it only happens once or twice is debatable. However, if you have always helped your toddler to sleep, he may well not have the resources to sleep on his own, and going 'cold turkey' like this is unfair and unreasonable.

If your toddler has always slept well, and is now just playing up because he is really testing your boundaries, letting him cry it out might well work, as long as you feel you understand why your toddler is being difficult about bedtimes, and you are prepared to explain to him what you are doing.

A better strategy might be to do this softly, softly rather than all or nothing. For example, if he won't stay put, insist he stays in his bed, but stay with him, perhaps the first time you can cuddle or rock him, then the next evening you can just sit next to the cot with your hand in it, stroking him, then gradually withdrawing your hand but still sitting next to him, then moving to the door, to standing outside the door, and so on.

Or if the problem is just getting into bed in the first place, start his bedtime routine later in evening when he is more likely to settle, and then gradually move bedtime forward.

Rewarding good bedtime behaviour

If your toddler is capable of understanding this, then you can go for the reward system. Let him have a special treat next day for staying in his own bed all night, or for not waking you up and so on. For a reward to be effective, it has to be meaningful and understandable. A two-year-old will not be able to cope with 'if you stay in bed every night this week, we will take you out at the weekend' – it's all just too big. But 'if you stay in bed in the morning and play quietly until Mummy comes in to see you, you can have a comic book when we go shopping in the morning' is just about doable. If you go down this route you must be prepared to withhold said treat next day if he does not earn it, so don't offer as a reward, something you were intending to do anyway.

With older children, star charts can be effective. One star for getting into bed by 7 p.m., another for staying in bed until 7 a.m., and so on, adding up over a week to a reward for ten stars say at the end of the week.

If they 'fail' on occasion, don't berate them – you can even empathize with them, 'What a shame, no star today! Never mind, I'm sure you can manage one tonight!'

Help! I had a bad dream! Dealing with night waking

Toddlers often start night waking even if they were good sleepers before, and often develop night terrors. It is no good telling him it was 'just a bad dream'; to him it was real and toddlers find it hard to distinguish reality from fantasy, imagined terrors from real ones. Instead, respond to the nightmare at face value, doing whatever you think will reassure your child. For instance, if he says there was a monster, tell him you have sent it away and locked the door and now it can't get back in.

If he's having frequent nightmares, consider how much stimulation he gets in the late afternoon and early evening. If he watches TV, choose a soothing, calming DVD, or better still, read a gentle story. Keep a diary to see if you can detect a pattern to the nightmares. Do they happen on nursery days? Are they related to potty training? Any major changes such as moving house, or you starting work, may affect his sleep. If he is ill or teething you can expect unsettled nights. Remember, no one's child sleeps through every night, so be calm, persevere, and he will sleep through again.

Signs of teething are drooling, runny nose, rash on chin, red cheeks, rejecting breast or bottle, wanting to suck more, nappy rash.

Some children who have become used to falling asleep with Mum or Dad in the room, will feel abandoned if they wake in the night. If this applies to your toddler, you will probably have to go down the 'softly softly' route to teach him to fall asleep on his own.

Other toddlers won't sleep through the night if they've learnt that something nice – like food or a long cuddle, happens if they wake up. Start cutting any 'night treats' down. Instead of rushing in to cuddle him, reassure your child from the doorway of his bedroom. Substitute water for middle of the night milky drinks – water is not really worth waking up for.

Is it morning yet? Dealing with early risers

What can you do with the child who wakes bright as a button, but too early? All human beings experience shallow sleep in the early hours, but we grown-ups are used to falling asleep again. Your baby could fall asleep again, but if he is over-stimulated, he will force himself to stay awake. Consider the following:

- Is he getting too much stimulation in the day, so he has too much to think about in the early hours?
- Is his bedroom too stimulating?
- Perhaps his bedroom needs to be darker.

If he's persistently being an early bird, you could put a few restful toys, like teddies or soft books, in his cot to play with when he wakes so he will be content until you are ready to face the day!

Bedroom versus playroom

A bedroom is your child's personal space, and it is tempting to keep all his toys in there – if only to keep the rest of the house feeling sane, but if a bedroom is too stimulating, your child will find it hard to get to sleep or to stay asleep. Think about keeping toys in another part of the house, or tidying them away in large, plain cupboards so your toddler can't see them from his cot.

Expected sleep patterns

It's not at all unusual for toddlers to wake during their night-time sleeps. A national survey of English mothers found that a quarter of one-year-olds were still waking during the night at least five nights a week. How your toddler naps during the day will affect his ability to sleep at night. If he is having difficulty falling asleep at bedtime, then it's worth having a think about the quality and quantity of his day-time naps.

By one year, your toddler will need about two day-time naps and a long period of sleep at night; by two years, he will probably only have one day-time nap, but this will still be a reasonably long one; anywhere between one and three hours. At three years, he may still want about an hour after lunch.

- Is he napping too late in the afternoon?
  Try to let him sleep no later than 3 p.m. if you want a bedtime around 6 p.m. or 7 p.m.
- Is he sleeping for too long in the day? Or perhaps, not long enough!
  Ironically, if your toddler does not get the sleep he needs during the day, he might be over-tired by bedtime and too cranky to settle well.

Case history: Catherine and Andrew

'Andrew is now 18 months old and has always woken every two hours during the night; from birth really, he has never slept more than two hours. Initially I breastfed him back to sleep, but once he was weaned I would go and cuddle him, and give him a milky drink until he fell back to sleep. I'm sure he can't really be hungry, but he always drinks it all up. I've got used to it, but now I am pregnant again I know I won't be able to cope with getting up for two children.

Answer: Children often continue to wake at night for feeds long after they need these nutritionally. If they are used to being fed back to sleep, they may well need this feeding. In this case it would be very harsh to go cold turkey as Andrew has never learnt to fall asleep on his own.

The first step is to increase the amount that Andrew is eating and drinking during the day to ensure that he really does get enough nutrition in 24 hours. Next it would be best to give him water when he wakes; milk is worth waking for, water is not. Also Catherine's partner could go to him during this transition period as Andrew may well associate Catherine with milk, but is unlikely to associate Dad with milk. Perhaps this could happen over a long weekend. If he is still waking, then the 'softly softly' approach could come in here – first night cuddles, second night stroking without lifting out of the cot, etc.

In situations like this it is really worth keeping a sleep diary for two weeks to see what patterns you can notice, and show it to an experienced outsider like your health visitor; ask what they think you could do.

Other sleep thoughts

- Don't send your toddler to bed for being naughty; that way bed becomes associated with unpleasant things.
- Some toddlers are better sleepers than others and things change over time anyway – don't be tempted to compare your toddler with your friends' children.
- If you are over-tired it's harder to be consistent, and consistency is really important with toddlers! Make sure you get enough sleep yourself; if necessary lie down after lunch when he does.
- A tired and irritable child is harder to deal with, so try to pre-empt this by starting the bedtime routine before he gets grouchy.

How you feel

Some sleep difficulties result from issues about the relationship between your child and you as parents, in particular feelings about separation. How you feel about the issue of responding to your toddler, particularly at night, may well be influenced by how you were treated yourself. Were you 'left to cry'? If you were, and if you can remember this, it may be that for you, the idea of your toddler crying, even for a couple of minutes, is abhorrent. There is a chance, of course, that if your partner is of similar age, background and culture; his parents may have read the same books as your parents, and he may therefore have had a similar upbringing. There is also the possibility that he will feel the same as you do. On the other hand, perhaps your partner's memories are of being secure, warm and nurtured. Perhaps he would like to offer this experience to his own children, but then again, having had his needs met, he may feel less distressed by his toddler's cries and may be more willing to follow advice which suggests leaving him to cry.

Both of these approaches will evoke a strong reaction in both of you, and it's important for your relationship that you and your partner know what you are doing and why. Try to discuss how you feel about sleep issues when you are both alert and functioning, rather than at 2 a.m. when all you want to do is to sleep!

Summary of this chapter

- Sleep is an issue for many toddlers, even if it has not been an issue before.
- Make sure your toddler gets plenty of sleep, both at night and during the day.
- A good bedtime routine will help your toddler get off to sleep.
- Many toddlers get night terrors which lead to night waking.
- Try rewarding good behaviour, and gradually weaning your toddler off needing you in the night rather than leaving him to 'cry it out'.
- Make sure you and your partner agree on your response to night waking.

section two

how your
toddler
develops

Introduction

So far we have looked at how your toddler behaves and what to do about it. In Section two, which is the main part of this book, we shall look at why he behaves the way he does, and try to understand more about his psychological development and your role in creating a new human being.

In Part one, we look at how your toddler develops socially and emotionally; how he relates to his family and the outside world; what effect his parents, siblings and friends have on him; and how he learns to become a social human being, being aware of others' emotions and feelings, and learning to behave and to conform to social norms. We look at how to keep your relationship healthy in order to raise a healthy toddler, and we discover how you can help him to make friends and fit in with other children.

Toddlers learn mostly through play, so Part two focuses on what play is, why it is important, and looks at how play helps your toddler develop creatively, intellectually and physically. We look at active play, which includes things like rough and tumble, climbing, running and, later on, interactive games like chase and football; all of which help your child's physical development and co-ordination. We also look at creative play – helping your toddler with drawing and painting for instance, and we explore what imaginative play is, how it works, and what it does for your toddler. Finally we look at the role of books, TV and computers in your toddler's life, and also the role of formal education; nursery and school as well as forms of childcare and how these might impact on your toddler psychologically.

The last part of this section focuses on cognitive development – how your child learns to think, speak and remember things, and how he becomes self-aware. How, in fact, he becomes a unique human being.

For those who have developmental concerns there is a short section at the end which explains what the main developmental disorders are, how you might spot them even at this young age, and more importantly, the useful and straight forward things you can do to minimize any problems, through diet and play.

All of this section draws on years of psychological research, trying to summarize the main findings down into information that is useful and practical. There are some suggestions for further reading if your interest has been sparked, but hopefully you will find all that you need to know to help your toddler within these pages. Enjoy!

part one

one

social and emotional development *

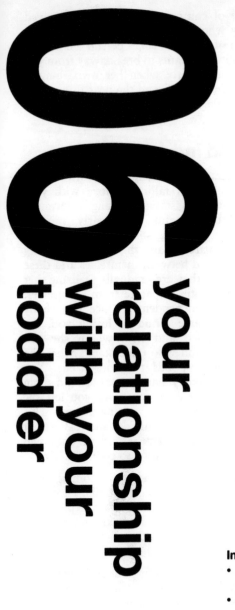

06 your relationship with your toddler

In this chapter you will learn:
- how your baby changes as she gets older
- why your toddler might affect your relationship with your spouse/partner
- how your family structure affects your toddler.

Your toddler is a bundle of contradictions. She has changed from that amenable baby who smiled when she saw you and who could not get enough of you, to a small person who seems to be in torment. One minute she wants to break away from you and do her own thing (particularly when her own thing is something you don't want her to do!) and the next minute she is clinging to you like a baby monkey.

Love, security and independence

It may be helpful to understand what is happening for her. As a baby, she spent her early months falling in love with you, bonding with you – what psychologists call 'making her primary attachment' to you. Babies spend their early months communicating non-verbally with one, sometimes two people, usually one or both of their parents, and this close interacting creates and strengthens the bond between themselves and these adult figures. At the same time they are gradually realizing that these adult figures exist as entities separate from themselves, that they can come and go independently. Once your baby grasped this concept, she became afraid of losing you, the person with whom she bonded and with whom she can communicate so easily, the person who understands what she wants and needs, and who responds to those needs. You probably noticed 'separation anxiety' emerging at around seven or eight months old; your baby cried whenever you left the room, having been quite happy about parting before. This developed into 'fear of strangers'; not only did she realize that you come and go, but she also became afraid of unknown people with whom she does not know how to communicate.

This was all happening at a time when she was becoming more in control of her body and beginning to get mobile. Of course this mobility gives her so many opportunities to explore the world, and she is driven to get out there and explore, but then at the same time this fear of losing you drives her back to be in close proximity to you. And therein lies the conflict.

The more secure your toddler feels about your love, the more she is able to move away from you and be independent. It is human nature; if you feel absolutely secure in your love for another person and are able to trust them completely, then you feel happy about them going away from you from time to time. You will miss them for sure, but you are not anxious that they are leaving you for good or that they won't come back.

So the more love and affection you shower on your toddler, the more secure she will feel and the more independent she will become. The idea that being over-affectionate, over-responsive, will 'spoil' your baby and make her emotionally dependent is actually the complete opposite of what happens in reality.

Consistency is really important too. Again think about how you feel. A person who is completely unpredictable is difficult to trust. If your toddler never knows how you are going to be, how you are going to respond, then she cannot feel secure and will actually cling to you more, as she feels anxious and uncertain.

Case history: Anne, Jack and Susanna

Anne and Jack lived together for nine months before Anne got pregnant. They got married just after Susanna was born. The first year went well – Anne stayed at home and looked after Susanna, Jack helped out around the house, taking over the cooking and many household chores.

Now Susanna is mobile, Anne finds her much harder work. When Susanna is naughty or throws a tantrum, Anne tries to get Jack to help, but as she sees it, Jack just 'gives in' to Susanna, whereas Jack thinks Anne is too strict. The result is that they both end up arguing, and Susanna seems to be making things worse, by playing up when they are both around.

Answer: Because Jack was not as involved with Susanna in the first year, it is easier for him to play 'good parent' and ignore Susanna's behaviour. He must recognize that his partner needs his help and back up. Meanwhile Anne needs to let Jack become more involved. Perhaps she could go out for the day on her own and leave Jack in charge. He needs to find his own way to parent Susanna.

It is also very important that Anne and Jack take time out together to talk through these issues and agree to support each other. They should either sit down in an evening when Susanna is in bed, and really talk this out or, if this is not possible, then arrange a babysitter so they can go out for the evening.

They need to identify the flashpoint; which sorts of behaviour in Susanna trigger these conflicts? Then they need to agree on a consistent response – it might be that Anne can relax a bit, or perhaps Jack needs to toughen up a bit. Either way, they must agree on boundaries, and then both agree to enforce them in the same way.

Toddlers affect relationships

Most people become parents as part of a couple, but nowadays that can mean many things. Only 60 per cent of people are married when they become parents, 25 per cent are cohabiting, and for the other 15 per cent some are separated or divorced, others are closely involved, still others are 'just friends'. Having a baby can put an immense strain on a relationship, so if the parents are still getting to know each other as a couple, or are not particularly committed before they have a baby, statistically speaking they may be less likely to be together by the time the baby becomes a toddler (94 per cent of married couples will still be together a year after the baby is born, 75 per cent of cohabiting couples will still be together, but of those who were only 'romantically involved' before the baby arrived, 48 per cent will no longer be together).

Being aware that babies put a strain on your relationship will certainly help, as you can be prepared for the occasional rocky ride. Many couples find it hard to consolidate their own relationships at the same time as taking on this new role of parent, so if you and your partner are fairly new to each other when you find yourselves becoming parents, it is helpful to be aware of this and make sure you follow the suggestions below for keeping the channels of communication open.

While mothers tend to become disenchanted with the relationship during the first year after the baby's birth, for the father, disenchantment sets in during the second year of the baby's life. However, the effect on the father of feeling dissatisfied with his partner is that he becomes less involved with his child, and this can generate a negative spiral in that the less involved he is, the more the mother resents him; he picks up on this and feels even more unhappy with his partner, so he becomes ever-more distanced from the toddler, and so on.

So the toddler years are often a time when relationships are under strain, especially if you have different feelings about what is acceptable behaviour from your toddler. You will find that looking after a toddler is something that challenges both of you, and your relationship needs to be strong. Consistency becomes really important and this depends on good communication. It is important that you don't become 'good parent, bad parent' where one is responsible for telling off, the other does all the cuddling, comforting and good stuff. Inconsistency is not good for your child either, as she will become confused about what is expected, and also unwittingly create more disharmony in your relationship as she plays up to your different roles. So make time for each other, keep the channels of communication open. Make a pact to regularly tell each other how you feel – it's not enough to just talk about mundane things like whose turn it is to take out the rubbish – this is not the sort of communicating you need to do to keep your relationship happy and flourishing.

Some suggestions:

- Get a babysitter once a fortnight and get out of the house for a meal together. You may know people with an au pair who would like to earn some extra cash. Local colleges often have trainee nannies who would welcome the money and the hands-on experience! Babysitting circles are a good idea, where you take turns with other new parents to babysit; the NCT may have a babysitting circle in your area, or you could form one from your mother and toddler group. Ring 0870 444 8707 for your local NCT branch.
- Ask grandparents to take your toddler away for a few hours so you can spend time being a couple again.
- Take turns to have a lie in on Sunday morning and recharge your batteries.
- Ask your partner for what you need.
- Don't expect your partner to do everything around the house in the same way you do, but be grateful to each other for the help.
- Make regular time together to talk about how parenting feels, and to agree strategies. A problem shared is far easier to deal with.

Difference between mothers and fathers

Some men find it easier to relate to their children once they begin to speak, and so may become more involved when their baby becomes a toddler. While men and women are equally capable of bringing up children, they do bring slightly different approaches to parenting, and women will tend to be 'nurturers' – seeking to connect, be intimate with and respond to their children while men tend to be 'encouragers' – stressing the importance of children's independence and encouraging risk-taking behaviour. While these are both equally valid approaches, problems might arise when one parent values their own approach over the other.

Consistency then, is not saying that you and your partner must act the same, but that you both need to value what the other does. As your children get older, having one parent who is cautious and another who pushes them into trying new things is no bad thing – you will balance each other out. Try to do what feels right for you, and don't be tempted to tell your partner how to parent – both styles will give your toddler different things. Consistency is about supporting and valuing each other's differences, but agreeing on boundaries and both being prepared to enforce these.

Effects of family breakdown

If the worst comes to the worst and your relationship does end, what is most important is to try to minimize the impact on your toddler. While children with behaviour problems are more likely to come from a non-traditional family structure, it's the stress within the family that creates problems, not the make-up of the family itself. Conflict between parents is stressful for children, whatever the outcome; if parents stay together and fight this is stressful for children, if they separate and divorce it is also stressful. Children can cope with different family structures such as parents living apart, as long as there is no conflict. If you can part amicably and keep communication channels open between your partner and your toddler, even though this is extremely hard to do, in the long term it will be of immense benefit. Children are resilient and can cope with most major changes as long as they feel secure; you can provide that security with extra love and attention during difficult periods.

Boys are generally more susceptible than girls to psychological stress, and therefore they may be more vulnerable when the family breaks up, probably because boys are not as skilled at communicating their feelings and tend to keep their worries to themselves. If your relationship is ending or in crisis, make sure your toddler, boy or girl, has plenty of opportunity to express any worries, and talk to them as much as you can about what is happening in a calm and matter of fact way.

• Raising a child in a single-parent family is not a problem in itself; your child will accept whatever family structure she is born into, as long as it is consistent, stable and loving. The issues are more about having enough time for your child; if you are sole breadwinner it can be hard to also find the time that your toddler really needs from you.

- Having to be Dad and Mum might seem problematic, but again most children will be happy with one parent as long as you can give them time and love. The hardest thing is lack of adult company and support, so try to make sure your social network includes other parents with children of a similar age with whom you can share issues and concerns.

- Even if your relationship with your partner breaks down completely, try to keep both sets of grandparents involved with your toddler.

- If you are forming a new relationship then expect your toddler to play up as she pushes the boundaries. Be firm but fair, and keep letting her know that she is loved. Remember she is unhappy about the changes and may well feel you are about to leave too.

Summary of this chapter

- Toddlers are in conflict; wanting to explore the world but being afraid of parting from you.

- Separation anxiety and fear of strangers are natural stages that babies go through on the way to becoming toddlers, and indicate that your baby has bonded well with you and feels confident in communicating with you.

- Children who are clingy often feel insecure in their parents' love. The more your children know they are loved, the more independent they can be.

- Consistency in parenting toddlers is really important. You need to be consistent yourself, and you and your partner need to agree on boundaries.

- Mothers and fathers bring different approaches to parenting, both equally valid, and you need to respect each other's styles.

- Having a toddler creates friction in family relationships, so it is important you take time to keep your relationship strong.

07

your toddler's position in the family

Having considered the impact of your toddler on your relationship with your partner in the previous chapter, perhaps the idea of having another baby is the last thing on your mind! But then if you do intend to have more than one child, you are probably wondering if there is an ideal age gap? This chapter looks at the implications of the various age gaps, as well as the effect on your toddler of having siblings, and whether the order in which you were born really does affect you.

The new sibling – your toddler's perspective

Babies need to form attachments to (bond with) at least one primary care-giver, usually their mother. Just meeting their physical needs is not enough; babies need cuddles, interaction and huge amounts of attention in their first two, even three years. It is rare that they are happy to accommodate another, younger baby, so if you have a small age gap you will need to ensure that both children get lots of love and attention from you.

As they get mobile, a well-attached child can become increasingly independent. When he knows that his mother is focused on him, ready to respond, he is likely to be happy playing some distance away, and in that respect it can look as if he is emotionally independent too. However, if he feels she is not paying him attention, or if she tries to push him away, he will cling. For most young children, the mere sight of Mum holding another baby is enough to elicit strong attachment behaviour. So most toddlers are likely to respond to a new arrival with regressive and clingy behaviour. You will need to be patient and understanding if your toddler behaves like this; don't worry, he will soon adapt when he knows that he still has your love.

After three years of age, children become less clingy, better able to accept their mother's absence and their peer group becomes more important. Four-year-olds bond with children of the same age, and prefer to spend time with them. Children above four years are able take on the role of responsible older sibling, rather than jealous rival for their mother's attention. In addition, four-year-olds naturally interact with babies as dependents, speaking motherese – the special high-pitched language for infants – see Chapter 19. So some mothers find that these years are a time when children accept a new baby more readily.

Your toddler – the new sibling's perspective

However, from the point of view of the new arrival, when they are somewhere between six and 18 months old, they become able to make multiple attachments, particularly with older siblings, and strong multiple attachments can make a baby more secure. With a small age gap your children will be together in a day nursery, and children settle better in day-care if they have a sibling around. From the baby's point of view, therefore, a small age gap is a great benefit.

No easy answer

To complicate matters, relationships will also change over time. The two- and four-year-olds who get on well together could equally hate each other when they are three and five! Same sex children quarrel more; different sexes will have less in common. As you can see, there isn't really an ideal age gap, and it is down to when you and your partner feel ready to take on this extra responsibility. It is worth talking to each other about the kind of family you both want. Do you like the idea of a lively household, with children who are close in age being able to play together? Or do you prefer the idea of giving each child lots of individual attention yourselves? Try to make the decision based on your own ideals rather than being influenced by pressure from outside.

Case history: Sarah, David and Edward

Sarah's children, David and Edward, were born 14 months apart, and are now aged four and five.

'Edward was colicky, so I'd just got through those first difficult months to find I was pregnant again! However, he was still sleeping a lot in the daytime when David, who was fortunately an easy baby, was born. I was also lucky that my husband worked locally and would arrive home at that dreadful time – 6 p.m. He took Edward off for a bath and cuddles. My Mum, Dad or sister also popped round to help in the afternoons. I would have really struggled otherwise.

I was very careful about Edward's feelings. When he came in for his morning cuddle, I made sure that David was never in the bed

– he was always in his crib. I would get David fed and comfortable, so the rest of the time was for Edward. I think Edward doesn't feel usurped because he can't ever remember being by himself.

I would say to anyone having a small gap like this – it's hard work, but don't worry about it. There are practical difficulties, but I don't regret it. They're great mates – maybe because they're both boys and like to play the same things. I have friends who are only now having their second – they're starting all over again, while I've moved on. We can do things together as a family, we can plan a day out that everyone will enjoy.'

While the four+ age gap is less common in our society, it is actually what nature intended. Anthropologists and historians reckon that children should be spaced four to five years apart through the contraceptive effect of normal long-term breastfeeding. As women leave motherhood later these days, the larger age gap becomes less possible. Interestingly the effects of birth order only applies when the age gap is less than five years, so as far as our prehistoric ancestors were concerned, birth order did not affect personality in the way it does today.

We tend now though, after two or three generations, to think that '2.2 children', two+ years apart, is the norm, while a small age gap (with both children being under two) is not unusual, when in fact either scenario is unusual both historically and culturally.

Considerations – small gap

- It's hard work. You may be woken in the night by two children, they will both be in nappies, and neither will be able to fend for themselves much – it will be like having twins.
- It's expensive; you will need two cots and a double buggy. You can't hand things down, so toys like bikes need to be shared or duplicated.
- It takes your body at least a year to recover from pregnancy and birth, so you may feel more tired after the second birth than you did first time around.
- The relationship between children with a small gap, especially if there are only two of them, can be very intense. Family squabbles and fallings out are common.

- However, lots of other people will go for the same age gap as you, so your family may find it easy to mix with other families.
- Your children will always have someone to play with of a similar age.

Considerations – large gap

- A large age gap drags out those early days for quite a while.
- Although older child can help, its tempting to rely on them too much – they are still entitled to their childhood!
- Even when older siblings are teenagers, they may still need you to mother them, especially if they've been used to being an only child.
- Children with larger age gaps are less likely to play together or to enjoy the same kinds of activities and holidays.
- You are less likely to experience sibling rivalry in the early days.
- You will have more time to enjoy them as babies.

Case history: Anne, William and Daniel

Anne had her two boys, William and Daniel, exactly two-and-a-half years apart 'to the day'. They are now three and five.

'We planned the gap very carefully. I wanted William to be able to feed himself, be potty trained and to be out of the cot by the time the new baby arrived.

They do fight a lot, but since Daniel turned two, they've been able to play together. William plays imaginative games like pirates, and co-opts Daniel, which he couldn't do before. Daniel follows William everywhere – 'me and my shadow'; William gets a bit fed up with it sometimes.

I think the gap has made Daniel very competitive. He always insists he's a big boy, even with children his own age, although he doesn't mind playing at being a baby for William.

The biggest regret I have about choosing this age gap is that William had his babyhood cut short. If he'd been smaller, he wouldn't have noticed, but at two, he was still really a baby who suddenly had to compete. I was also handicapped at first as I didn't have a double pushchair, so we could only ever go as far as William could walk.'

Sibling relationships

Having a sibling makes children more aware of others; being forced to interact on a daily basis with someone of a similar age gives your child social interaction skills and will help him to grow up with a more complex understanding of social relationships and of other people's points of view. Eighty per cent of children have siblings usually only a few years older or younger than themselves, and while some children can be very tolerant of younger siblings, others can be at best ambivalent, at worst hostile, and these reactions happen in all societies throughout the world.

Babies who grow up with a hostile sibling are more likely to be anxious, depressed or aggressive as adolescents. Also if children think that their sibling receives more attention and affection, they are more likely to be aggressive or difficult. So it really does matter, and getting the relationship off to a good start is important. One study showed that children who were aged between one and three years when their younger sibling was born, and who showed friendly interest and concern for the new baby in the first three weeks of his life, were more likely to show concern if their sibling was hurt or distressed at a follow-up six years later.

When your new baby arrives you may well feel tired and over-stretched, but it will be important that you encourage your toddler to get on well with the new baby from day one.

Effects of birth order

Another way siblings can influence each other is by the order in which they are born. Psychologists have found some general trends linking birth order to personality, though other factors, like coming from a stable family background, are often far more important. As the effect of birth order is partly down to how you act towards your children, if you consciously choose to act differently, you can minimize the effects. Size of family and gap between siblings is important too; if there is a gap of five or more years between children, it will be as if you have started a second family, so the next new baby will have the characteristics of first-born children. This is probably because their older sibling is more adult-like than child-like. The sex of the child is important as well; a girl born after several boys may be treated as more 'special' for instance.

Children from large families generally make friends easily and are more tolerant. If you are one of several siblings, you get to see your parents in a more complete and human light than only-children, and are likely to develop a more rounded view of other people and to have more natural self-confidence in superficial relationships.

First-born

Being first-born (with younger siblings born within five years)

The oldest child tends to be more intelligent, achievement-orientated, and is often conformist – they like to do the right thing. However, they may also feel more anxious and insecure. This is probably because initially they have lots of adult attention, but then feel insecure when a later child is born, feeling they miss out on the parental attention that they have become accustomed to. Now they try to win approval from parents and strive to achieve.

As parents you may find you use your oldest child as an additional pair of hands, so he may feel a higher sense of responsibility, and may feel less carefree than later-born children. Some parents feel very protective and indulgent towards their first-born child, but other parents can be harsher and set higher standards for the first-born than they do for later children.

The middle child

Being the middle child (if surrounded by siblings with less than a five year gap either side)

Children born within two years of an older sibling are not close enough to feel completely equal, but close enough to try to compete. They often grow up to be extremely competitive and driven people. They are the sibling most likely to protest and rebel. Second children with a two-year or more age gap are less driven, more spontaneous and easy-going, more tactful, adaptable, patient and relaxed than their older sibling. They can't hope to win, so they become less competitive and more adaptable. They often succeed in life in more eccentric ways.

Traditionally being the middle child is seen as a difficult position; initially these children have to share their parents' attention with an older sibling, and when a younger sibling arrives, there is even more competition for even less parental time.

Common characteristics of a middle child can be: skilled mediator, avoids conflict, independent, strong orientation to peer group with lots of friends.

The youngest child

Being the youngest child (with sibling no older than five years)

Youngest children are better at understanding people, and the more brothers and sisters they have, the more skilled they become. Having older siblings teaches children about human nature. The youngest child tends to be more charming, less ambitious and less domineering. Occasionally they may feel inadequate or inferior, but usually possess enough charm to get their way.

You may be more relaxed with your youngest baby; you know what you are doing now, and being relaxed, you will probably put less pressure on this child. The youngest also benefits from living in a child-friendly environment, having older siblings to learn from as well as adults.

The only-child

Only-children tend to be very successful, as well as more imaginative. They appear mature for their age, as they are used to interacting with adults. Only-children are the most likely to create imaginary companions, and may grow up to be less skilled at small talk.

The only-child is similar in some ways to the first-born, and they start life the same way, but the only-child never has the challenge of adapting to siblings. They may be more adult in their behaviour, but may also be more self-centred and impatient.

Only-children, like first-borns, tend to be more conscientious, more socially dominant, less agreeable, and less open to new ideas; however, only-children do not seem to be any less sociable. It also seems to be the case that only-children are high achievers and have above average IQ scores, though interestingly, not as high as first-borns; typically two or three points lower than an oldest child with one or two younger siblings.

This seems to contradict the idea that first-borns or only-children are benefiting from extra parental attention. If this were true, then only-children would be more intelligent than first-borns. Instead it looks as if first-borns benefit from the extra stimulation involved in teaching their younger siblings.

Summary of this chapter

- There is no easy answer to the question, 'What is the ideal age gap?'
- It is important that the relationship between your toddler and the new baby gets off to a good start.
- Birth order has some effects on personality, but a lot will depend on how you respond to your toddler too.

08

the development of emotional control

In this chapter you will learn:
- about the development of emotions in your toddler
- how temperament and personality emerge
- how your toddler moves towards emotional independence
- how to help your toddler develop self-esteem.

Human beings the world over experience certain emotions in the same way as each other and can recognize when other people are feeling those same emotions by their facial expressions. These so-called primary emotions – happiness, interest, surprise, sadness, fear, anger and pain – are our shared human inheritance, whether we are born in Greenland or Australia. You probably noticed that your toddler felt and expressed these emotions from birth and recognized these same emotions in you.

These emotions are hard-wired into our primitive brains and would exist if we learnt nothing else about our world, but through time, in order to fit in with our particular society, we need to develop more elaborate emotions which will encourage us to behave unselfishly, to fit in with other people. These 'secondary' emotions, like pride, shame or guilt, as well as the more complicated empathy and sympathy, depend on knowledge and understanding of other people and their point of view, and so they also require self-consciousness. Toddlerhood is the time when these begin to emerge, as your child develops a sense of self and an awareness of others (see Chapter 21).

Why self-conscious emotions develop later

Secondary emotions can only develop as your toddler's brain grows capable of experiencing them, which is not until the frontal cortex of the brain matures. The frontal cortex eventually tells us what not to do; it stops us punching people if they annoy us for instance, but this is still growing in the early years of a child's life.

As we saw in Chapter 01, experiences which are repeated over and over create stronger connections in the brain. In the case of emotions, positive experiences, particularly in the first year of life, help the frontal cortex to grow and connect up. So as your child moves into the toddler years, experiences of being parented with love, but also with boundaries, help your child to develop these self-conscious emotions, which also make her want to exercise self-control and behave in the way society expects.

Several parts of the developing cortex seem to be responsible for emotional development and, eventually, emotional control in your toddler. For instance, the orbitofrontal part of the prefrontal cortex starts to mature around ten months when your baby begins to turn into a toddler, although it will not function fully until she is about 18 months old and this part of the frontal cortex specializes in recognizing faces. It seems likely that this helps your child remember 'emotionally loaded images' – for instance a look of disapproval on your face when she does something you don't want her to do. So initially she will control her impulses because you are there telling her not to do something, but eventually the memory of your facial expression when she does something wrong will be enough to inhibit that behaviour; the memory will trigger that secondary emotion of shame, and your child will draw on this memory to regulate her behaviour – it becomes, if you like, her conscience.

Developing emotional self-control

Helping your toddler to develop emotional self-control will actually benefit her in many other ways. One psychologist worked with a group of four-year-olds; each was given a marshmallow and told she could eat it now, in which case she would get only the one, or she could wait till the psychologist returned in 15 minutes in which case she would get a second one. The psychologist then left the room, and immediately some of the children ate the marshmallow, but the others managed to hold off with various strategies like squirming and fidgeting, talking to themselves or even covering up their eyes to stop themselves looking at the marshmallow! What was interesting (apart from what this says about psychologists and their own development of secondary emotions like empathy) was that the children who could control themselves at four years of age, who could exercise delayed gratification, got on better with their peers later in life and had better grades on leaving school than those who could not control themselves. Even more fascinating is that measuring the same children's IQs at age four did not predict their later academic success as well as the marshmallow experiment. The children's performance on the marshmallow test could predict their later academic achievements more accurately than IQ tests.

So where does this ability to delay gratification come from? It appears that the limbic system, the primitive part of the brain, is partly responsible. Children are born with particular tendencies to be more or less impulsive, but societal expectations can also mould this through time as the frontal cortex develops and places more or less emphasis on the need for self-control.

Your toddler's personality

For years and years, scientists have debated whether we are born with particular personalities or whether it is the world around us which shapes who we are. The answer is probably a mixture of both.

Babies are born with some aspects of their personality in place, the most obvious and fixed is what we call temperament; whether a baby is 'easy going' with a low arousal threshold (it takes a lot to startle her) or 'difficult' (easily startled, quick to cry at the slightest change in her environment). This low–high arousal continuum is pretty much there at birth and continues through the early months of life. It seems to be controlled by how reactive the amygdala is (which is the part of the limbic system responding to fearful situations). But of course how we react to this as parents is going to influence our babies' future personalities. Parents who respond to the difficult baby's needs, attempt to soothe her, to understand her, find that these babies become calmer and more settled in time, though they will probably tend to be shyer children, more inhibited in new situations. And it is interesting to think that we are viewing these babies through a fairly judgemental lens. Why is high arousal 'difficult' and low arousal 'easy'? Only because we judge it to be so.

A society which values high emotionality, quick tempers and volatile responses might label our 'difficult' baby as 'strong' and our 'easy' baby as 'weak', for instance. In the West we also think that being shy or inhibited in social situations is not a good thing, and encourage our children to become more outgoing and uninhibited, whereas in Asian cultures social inhibitions are more valued. And if you compare the two cultures, there are more shy children in Asian cultures than Western cultures, which shows that even though children may have an inborn temperamental predisposition to be inhibited or uninhibited, by our responses to this trait, we can influence the final outcome of this, the most inborn aspect of our personalities.

How might this work in practice? If your toddler seems particularly fearful you would probably encourage her to take safe risks and to discover for herself that no harm comes from her experiments, for instance, encouraging her to go up the slide and come down with you holding her hand. After a few times of experiencing the pleasure of coming down, she will then be more willing to do it for herself. If, however, your toddler was particularly uninhibited, your response would be to warn her of danger, 'ooh, hot!' as she lurched towards the fire, or 'slowly!' as she raced towards the swing. A combination of your fearful response and a couple of bumps might well temper that recklessness a little bit. You can also see perhaps that how fearful you are is going to impinge on how fearful she is likely to become. If you are very fearful you will probably react negatively to the idea of her trying something slightly risky, and thus her fears will be reinforced.

Coping with shyness

So as we have seen, the tendency to be shy is probably inborn, maybe even inherited, and of course if you have shy parents you are probably more likely to be shy yourself from copying your parents' behaviour. There is nothing wrong with being shy; children who are socially inhibited often do very well academically, probably because they find schoolwork more rewarding than social interactions. And while uninhibited children may seem to be more sociable, extremely uninhibited children can actually struggle later on, perhaps becoming too aggressive and defiant within the constraints of school if their exuberance is not well challenged.

Most uninhibited children remain outgoing and the challenge for parents is to channel that energy and to set and maintain firm boundaries. But shy children can become more sociable with help:

- Gently encourage your toddler to push herself a little bit further than she initially seems to want to, whether in meeting new people or attempting new things.
- Don't push her too hard though. Go at her pace but just one step ahead.
- Introduce new people gradually and without fuss.
- Model outgoing behaviour. When you meet someone new or encounter a new situation, act confidently. Your toddler will be watching your response.
- Don't over-react to your child's shyness, as it then can become a way of getting attention. For instance, on meeting someone new, shy children should be firmly and quickly encouraged to respond to greetings. After this, let them out of the limelight and they will soon learn that being polite is not such an ordeal.

Mixing with other children

Large families are far less common now, and so toddlers have fewer opportunities to practise getting along with other children. She will need your help when discovering how to get along with her own age group. The child from a small family also has less of a crowd to hide in, so she will feel under far more pressure on social occasions.

You need to give her lots of opportunities to meet other babies and toddlers, and to allow her to gain social skills with her own age group. This becomes more important as she approaches nursery age, when she will have to cope without you.

> Your toddler will learn social behaviour through you. If you are shy and avoid saying hello or making eye contact, she will probably be shy as well. If instead you always greet other people as well as your toddler in a friendly manner, and make an effort to be polite, she will try to copy you. It will also help if you make social behaviour explicit to your toddler, but don't expect her to behave the way you tell her to, if you do the opposite yourself.

Mother and toddler groups are ideal places for practising social skills. Try to pick one that has similar activities and routines to the nursery she will eventually attend. (In fact, some nurseries do have mother and toddler groups attached.) But choose a group where the right signals are given. If it is a free for all, where parents ignore running battles, and there is a lot of unstructured running around, your toddler will learn the wrong social skills. Playgrounds and parks are the place for running around, but toddler groups should have lots of interesting, quiet activities where children, alongside watchful parents, can enjoy themselves as well as interacting with their peers. Ideally there should be more than enough toys so that no one needs to fight over anything.

Case history: Jackie and Diana

Jackie's daughter Diana is now two-and-a-half, and is an only-child. She is happy playing on her own or with Jackie, but does not like mixing with other children. She hates being left in the church crèche, and at the local playgroup she clings to Jackie's leg and refuses to try to play with the other children. Jackie feels fairly sympathetic; she remembers feeling painfully shy when she was a little girl, and feels that in the crèche and the playgroup, the large number of boys running around shouting and screaming is putting Diana off. Jackie is happy to continue letting Diana play on her own, but is worried about how she will cope at nursery school which she is due to start after her third birthday.

Answer: It does sound as if these environments would be a bit of a baptism of fire! Diana is used to a quiet house and familiar toys, so start one step at a time, invite unfamiliar children into the territory where Diana feels safe – her own home.

Ask the nursery for the names of one or two other children, probably girls, who will be starting nursery at the same time as Diana, and invite one of them round to play. Put away any really precious toys – it is unfair to expect Diana's first experiences of sharing to be with her favourite things. Instead, get out lots of bits and pieces that they can enjoy playing with together (for example, lots of cars on a big car mat, or dressing up clothes, or if you can cope with it, playdough or paints). If Diana copes well with this, progress to inviting perhaps two or three children round. The next step would be to take all the children out somewhere together, like the park, so they are on neutral territory. Try each time to progress a little further, but be prepared to retrench if Diana begins to feel too uncomfortable. She will probably cope admirably if she can take small steps towards sociability.

Self-esteem

How do children develop self-esteem? Self-esteem is about evaluating yourself against others; comparing your concepts of yourself to others. Self-esteem is going to have an effect on our emotional state, but also on how we perform in the world. There is some evidence that children with high self-esteem tend to be less conformist and more creative, and that highly creative children usually have a high level of self-esteem.

Children with high self-esteem tend to have parents with high self-esteem, unsurprisingly. They are more likely to be securely attached or bonded to their parents and to have experienced firm, fair and consistent treatment. To help your child develop self-esteem:

- only criticize your child's behaviour not your child herself
- provide her with challenges so she can succeed at something difficult, while choosing challenges which are not so hard that she is bound to fail
- if she succeeds, give generous but explicit praise afterwards, for example, 'you rode that tricycle really well. What great steering, you didn't bump into anything and you went so fast!'
- tell her that you love her and that you are proud of her and explain why. Be specific here, for example, 'I am so proud of you for saying thank you nicely just then'
- demonstrate your trust in her abilities by not intervening unless you really have to, for safety, and then explain why you have done so.

Developing independence

Linked to self-esteem is the ability to act independently of others. Adults with low self-esteem may be those who were insecurely attached at an early age; if they did not have a chance to be dependent as babies they may well still be seeking this dependency throughout life, whereas those who were allowed to be dependent are able to be independent later on.

One of the problems with our society placing high value on emotional independence and on being outgoing and self-sufficient, is that parents can often push their babies towards independence before they are ready. Many parents misguidedly push even young babies away, not cuddling them in case the baby 'gets spoilt'; not taking the baby into their own bed in case 'it creates a rod for our backs'. In fact the more a parent responds to a baby with closeness and affection, the more likely it is that the baby will grow up to be a secure, independent toddler.

The more secure that your toddler feels in your love, the more she can cope without it. So, for instance, when leaving your toddler it's important that you tell her when you are leaving, and reassure her that you will come back. Never sneak away without saying goodbye.

Once your toddler becomes mobile she may well seem to want to explore new situations and do her own thing, but this all depends on having you as a secure base to return to. Even though she looks independent, her self-confidence depends on you staying within easy reach. Emotionally she will alternate between clinging and independence for a long time.

Helping her to separate

Places like playgrounds, where she can feel a sense of exploration and achievement without danger, are very important for developing independence. You will soon learn what she is capable of doing on her own, and when she will need your support. When she looks unsure, often all she needs is your presence. If you remove her from a tricky situation, you will be denying her the chance to succeed eventually. Instead, encourage her attempts while keeping an open hand within grasping distance if needed.

A toddler who believes she is capable of doing things on her own is gaining self-confidence. You can help by creating an environment which makes independence easier, for instance, you can have coat pegs that she can reach herself, cupboards where her own things are kept that she can access easily. You can teach her basic tasks like washing her face, undressing, putting dirty socks in the basket, throwing rubbish in the wastepaper basket and so on. Remember to praise all her attempts, even if the results are not perfect!

Demonstrate your trust in her abilities by not intervening (unless you really have to, for safety, and then explain why you have done so). Let her choose her own clothes if she wants to, even if it offends your sense of colour!

Tasks for your toddler to try at different stages

(NB: All children progress at different rates. Don't push her before she is ready as you may demoralize her.)

	12–18 months	18–24 months	24–30 months
Feeding	Lifts cup, but can't replace without spilling. Wants to feed herself, but spoon usually turns upside down before reaching mouth. *Provide*: Finger foods and a no-spill trainer cup.	Can use beaker independently. Beginning to use fork. *Things you can do*: Get her own cutlery set. Eat with her; she will try to copy your table habits.	Eating competently. *Things you can do*: Involve her in preparing simple meals, from mixing ingredients to consuming the end product!
Movement	Starts to walk and crawls upstairs. *Things you can do*: Move 'cruising' furniture further apart, encouraging her to take a step. Show her how to crawl downstairs.	Moving fast, though in a straight line. *Provide*: Pedal-less sit-on toy. Devise a safe route without too much steering and away from steps.	Constantly on the go! *Provide*: Footballs, small steps to jump off. Set up an obstacle race.
Dressing	Co-operates with being dressed. May take off hat and shoes.	Removes an open coat. *Provide*: Dolls with easy clothes. Simple dressing-up items like shawls and floppy hats.	Undresses herself, beginning to get dressed, though not zips or buttons.

	Provide: Activity toys with zips, buttons, and dials to twiddle. Scribbling also helps manipulation skills.		*Provide*: Easy clothes with elastic waists and Velcro. These are better for potty training too!
Cleaning	Time to introduce a toothbrush. *What you can do*: Let her have a go, but follow this with 'my turn'. Use little or no toothpaste, as she will swallow it.	Introduce her to washing hands before meals and after going to the toilet. *What you can do*: Teach her to avoid the hot tap. Provide a footstool and an easily reached towel.	Now using potty – she may use toilet by herself. Will need help wiping her bottom. *What you can do*: Leave a toilet trainer seat and footstool in place. Let her flush the toilet herself.

Summary of this chapter

- Primary emotions – happiness, interest, surprise, sadness, fear, anger and pain – are present from birth. The secondary emotions – pride, shame or guilt – which depend on awareness of others, begin to develop in the toddler years.
- Emotional self-control, or the ability to delay gratification, develop in these early years and are a good predictor of later popularity and intelligence.
- While certain aspects of your toddler's personality are inborn, your response to her will also have an effect.
- Society seems to value certain personality types over others, and this will also influence how your toddler turns out.
- Independence is only possible when your toddler feels secure in her relationship with you.

09

learning to behave

In this chapter you will learn:
- why toddlers are so impulsive
- whether pre-school children can understand the difference between right and wrong
- how to help your toddler become altruistic.

Do you get the feeling that your toddler spends most of his day thinking of new ways to provoke you? Don't worry, you are not alone in feeling like this, and in fact there are perfectly logical reasons why toddlers spend many of their waking hours trying to do exactly what you do *not* want them to do.

Toddlers are in conflict; they want independence, they want to explore the world, but they also still depend on care-givers for love and security, and yet these same care-givers, who were offering unconditional love to them as babies, suddenly seem to be thwarting their attempts at independence. They feel pushed and pulled, and to cap it all, they can't articulate what they are feeling, as they are still operating on a fairly unconscious, un-analytical level.

What is happening in your toddler's brain

As we saw in Chapter 01, human babies are born nine months too early if we extrapolate from other, similar species like gorillas and chimpanzees. This prematurity is the result of evolving both a big head to contain a big brain and a narrow pelvis to walk upright; the only way to marry these two conflicting demands is to give birth earlier than usual. However, as we have also seen, being born early is an advantage in other ways, as it means each child can grow a brain to suit the particular demands of the environment into which he is born, thus allowing human beings to live in every conceivable habitat.

So your toddler's brain is doing its final development outside the uterus, in response to his world, and of course this mostly means in response to you. The first year of his life involved building up connections through experience, and as certain events occurred over and over again, the same group of neurons were activated simultaneously, and thus life became more predictable.

The last bit of the brain to really develop though is the top few layers of cells, that wrinkly surface called the cortex, and it is this bit of our brain which gives us language, reasoning, our ability to read books or solve crosswords – everything which separates us from the rest of the animal kingdom.

When your baby is born, the inner part of the brain is fully functional. This includes the brain stem which is responsible for things we have no control over, like breathing, heart rate, digestion, and reflexes, but also includes the hypothalamus which is responsible for regulating and maintaining systems and thus influences us unconsciously, making us find water when we are thirsty for instance. It also includes the amygdala which is responsible for our response to fear; the 'flight or fight' response. On top of that primitive brain grows the main structure of the brain, the cerebrum, which is responsible for unconscious emotional experiences and skills and which we share with the other mammals, and which is overlaid by the human cortex.

The front part of the cortex, which is responsible for things like self-control, is still growing after birth and connecting up for many years to come. We now believe that it is still being refined into our early twenties, which goes partly towards explaining why teenagers are still quite impulsive and why teenage boys are so prone to car accidents.

Of course, all parts of the brain are connected to some extent and work together at all times, but the difference with a toddler is the inability of the frontal cortex to stop impulsive behaviour.

The primitive part of his brain will register that he is holding something hot, and instinctively get him to pull his hands away. Now you as an adult could actually override that instinctive behaviour; having registered that in fact you're holding a valuable plate, your frontal cortex can override your primitive response, thus saving the plate from destruction. Your toddler would not be capable of doing this at all. But it makes sense that the frontal cortex develops in response to a social world which tells it what is important and what is not – whether plates matter for instance.

So in these early years, you may well be saying, 'no!' a lot, and may be restraining, disciplining, telling him off – basically setting, reinforcing and maintaining boundaries. But although this is exhausting and sometimes debilitating, it is what your toddler needs, over and over again, to build up levels of self-control to make him into a socially functioning human being, and Chapter 02 will hopefully have given you some practical ideas about making this work for you.

Case history: Amanda, Beatrice and Bethany

Amanda is mother to twins Beatrice and Bethany who are two-and-a-half years old. Amanda works part-time while the twins go to nursery. She finds trying to get them out of the house in the morning to drop them off and still get herself to work on time, a real battle, and she arrives at work stressed and exhausted. She usually parts from the twins on a bad note, which makes her feel terrible. The mornings are just a screaming fest with her struggling to put unco-operative feet into shoes, wriggling arms into coats, and pinning them into car seats against their will.

Answer: children do not have our sense of urgency; it's when you try to hurry that you will have the biggest confrontations. Also when children are tired or unhappy, they are most likely to dig their heels in, and in this situation they are being rushed to do something they probably don't want to do anyway. Amanda needs to have sensible expectations. Her children perhaps need longer to get ready and to adjust to a new day; she should start earlier, perhaps after an earlier bedtime. She could use a countdown – ten minutes to go, five minutes to go, etc., and offer them a reward if they are ready on time. It's best if it can become a fun race against time, perhaps with a big clock by the door to be the 'baddy', so you are all trying to beat the clock, not each other.

Learning right from wrong

So toddlers need to learn what behaviour is expected of them, and they can do this fairly quickly actually, but do they have a concept of right or wrong?

Psychologists know that even pre-school children have a fairly sophisticated grasp of right and wrong; they can distinguish between actions that break social conventions (not putting your belongings in the right place say) and moral conventions (not sharing, hitting). They know that some rules apply at school and some at home, and that some are more deserving of punishment than others. This sort of understanding is fairly sophisticated when you think about it, and means it is certainly worth explaining to your toddler why things are wrong and being explicit about morality. It also means your toddler will cope pretty well with changing rules in different places; for instance at playgroup he is allowed to do X, but not at home, and so on (though changing rules in the same place will confuse and unsettle him).

Altruism

One of the issues psychologists have struggled to understand is why people are altruistic. Why should we help others, especially when helping others puts our own lives at risk? Why, for instance, do people jump into rivers to save drowning strangers? And how does altruism develop?

It can be argued that helping others helps ourselves; it's like an unspoken rule that we all help each other and in the process we help our own DNA to survive. Evolutionary psychologists have developed quite complicated arguments to show how this might work in practice, which is beyond the scope of this book, but one of the minor flaws in their argument is that some people choose not to be altruistic. So given that we don't all leap into rivers – that there is an element of choice – it must mean that being altruistic is a learnt rather than instinctive behaviour. So do children start out being selfish and then learn altruism?

The first relationship and the development of altruism

We now think that babies are unconsciously learning the intrinsic value of being altruistic from a very early age through their first relationship with their primary care-giver (usually their mother). Human beings seem to have an inborn motivation to form relationships with each other based on co-operation (after all, human societies form in all parts of the world and there is evidence of communal living from pre-historical remains). Babies learn mutual trust, to give and receive, in early family interactions like playing peek a boo or in the interplay of mutual gaze. There is also evidence that if babies form insecure attachments with their parents, they are less likely to form trusting relationships when older and are also less likely to be altruistic.

How soon can children act altruistically?

From a young age, children demonstrate altruistic behaviour. For instance, we can often observe even very young children trying to comfort or help someone even without being asked. Are these children behaving altruistically because they have come to expect a reward for this type of behaviour, or are they genuinely acting out of regard for others? And what influences some children to act unselfishly while others do not?

One experiment set out to measure this. The experimenters put out a dish with a sign saying, 'Help poor children: marbles buy gifts.' Children aged six to ten were then given the chance to earn marbles in a game. The adult played the game first and either gave away half her marbles, exhorted the child to donate her marbles, did both or did neither.

The children were then left to play on their own but were secretly observed. What happened was that those children who had seen the adult donate her marbles were most likely to donate their own marbles. The preaching had some effect, but if the adult had not given her marbles away, the children were unlikely to do so. This suggests that children are more likely to *copy* altruistic behaviour than to be altruistic because they are *told* to act that way. Of course this experiment might have been measuring compliance rather than altruism per se, but it does suggest there is some truth in the claim that children will copy what you do, not what you say!

These were of course older children, and it is harder to work out what is going on with infants, but from psychologists' observations we can conclude that some children under 20 months of age do show an emotional response to other children's upset but often respond simply by getting upset *themselves*, whereas children who are aged between 20 and 30 months may attempt to comfort another child themselves.

This fits in with what we know about children's understanding of the world, in that, by two years of age, they can understand cause and effect and presumably therefore understand why their peers are upset. They also understand the difference between themselves and other people (see Chapter 21) so they understand that the upset belongs to someone else, rather than generally relating to a state of upset. Children who are younger than 20 months may be getting upset themselves as they do not have this understanding of life being different for someone else.

Teaching your toddler to be altruistic

However, altruism does not come naturally, parents have to teach their children about this, and we tend to do this without really thinking, rewarding our children with praise and affection when they act unselfishly, and exhorting them to help other children in trouble when appropriate. When children do not respond to others, parents tend to scold them or try to actively teach them what was going on. Very few mothers (only about eight per cent) ignore altruistic or lack of altruistic behaviour. Explaining the consequences of his behaviour to your toddler makes it more likely that he will become altruistic, but being punished for not acting socially does not appear to work.

> Interestingly, in societies where women contribute to the family money, children are more altruistic. This is because more household tasks are delegated to them and thus the children learn helpful behaviour early on. However, in traditional societies where competition is valued, children are less altruistic than in societies where co-operation is valued, even though the children in each society are treated with equal affection.

Children will learn by example, so it is important that you model good behaviour, but in addition, explaining right and wrong in situations is important. There is no point in punishing children if they don't behave altruistically, but lots of point in explaining why they should behave differently next time.

The development of empathy

Altruism is acting in response to someone else's situation, but often this is triggered by an underlying emotion – empathy. We saw in Chapter 08 that empathy is a secondary emotion, which develops in response to being part of a social world. How does this happen?

Parents who are empathic themselves and who respond sensitively to their children's needs are more likely to have children who are empathic to others. However, the child's own temperament also makes a difference; children who are temperamentally more impulsive and less able to regulate their own emotions (see previous chapter) are less empathic to others.

Perhaps when newborn babies imitate their parent's facial expressions, this is the beginning of empathy. Recognizing emotions in another's face and responding with a similar facial expression could certainly be seen as an early empathic response, though babies are not capable of empathy until they are fully conscious of other people and know that these other people can feel differently from themselves. However, even from birth, using the primitive limbic system, your baby is matching your facial expressions and feelings with his own feelings in the primitive emotional part of the brain, and we also know that autistic children, who cannot experience empathy, are often born with limbic deficits.

One experimenter looked at how the development of empathy might relate to the development of mind. She found that children who had a strong sense of self-recognition on the mirror test (see Chapter 21) also had stronger levels of empathy with others – they understood that the experimenter was 'sad' when her teddy's arm fell off.

Summary of this chapter

- Toddlers are in conflict; wanting to explore and wanting to be near you, and your reaction in trying to contain them adds to their confusion.
- Setting boundaries and enforcing discipline is about creating self-control in your child, and is a necessary part of helping your toddler to develop.
- From early on, children are learning about right and wrong, and are capable of developing altruistic behaviour and empathy, but are more likely to do this if you demonstrate altruistic behaviour yourself.

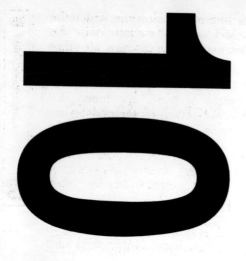

10

making friends

In this chapter you will learn:
- why friendships are important
- how friendship works at different ages
- what makes children popular.

So far we have looked at how your toddler develops within the family, but in this chapter we will look at the relationships she will make in the world outside – her friendships with other children.

Can toddlers make friends with each other?

It seems to be a commonly held belief that it is not until children reach school age that their peer groups become important. In fact, scientists have discovered that your child will be interested in other children from a very early age.

One study observed toddlers aged 12 to 18 months at play, watching where they looked and who they touched (who, therefore, they were in close proximity to) and found that the children mostly touched their mother but they spent more time looking at children of the same age as themselves than at anyone else in the room.

So your toddler will be very interested in other children, but because she is not socially skilled, she probably won't tend to make contact, as she doesn't know how. Instead you will probably notice that she looks at other children or makes some sort of noise at them; occasionally you will see her exchanging a smile with a child of a similar age or perhaps they might show each other a toy. Scientists have observed this sort of interacting happening every minute or so in toddler groups but it only lasts a few seconds because the children have not really grasped social interaction skills and can't follow these friendly overtures through. Under-twos also imitate each other a lot, and imitation is the beginning of social interaction.

What helps toddlers learn to interact?

Adults 'scaffold' social behaviour; this means that they build on any tentative interaction and actively teach the child what to do next, although it will not be until your toddler is between two and three years of age that she will be able to interact skilfully with children of the same age without this sort of help. Experience in mother and toddler groups or day nurseries can help, and once your toddler is able to interact socially with other children she will really benefit from nursery school.

When your toddler seems interested in a child her own age, you can help her learn these social skills. Say, for instance, 'Do you think that boy might like to play with us?' while giving the other child friendly signals or holding out your hand to indicate he should join in.

Then when they are together you will probably need to do all the work; initiating the action and making suggestions, 'Shall we build a train track? You could lay the track while Joey makes a station for the people to wait at...' and so on. Once they are involved in a joint activity, it is helpful to make explicit what is happening. 'Oh aren't you playing well together! You are both taking turns. You are helping each other. Shall we let Joey have a go now?'

Play and friendships

Children under two years tend to engage in 'parallel play' meaning they play alongside others without actually interacting, or they are 'onlookers' – watching other children at play. However, as they get older they start to be involved in associative or co-operative play; for instance, building a tower together, or actually helping each other with their activities. Outdoors, children can become more involved with each other, and you will find that they form bigger friendship groups as they get older. But imaginative or socio-dramatic play, which is so important for your toddler's cognitive development (see Chapter 15), often depends on having friends.

What friendships do for your toddler

Children prefer to play with those they know, and their play is more fruitful and more intricate, with known children. Even toddlers have more positive interactions with toys and show more complex play if they are playing with familiar children (see Chapter 15). By age three, children need friends to play with if they are to engage in imaginative play; they will not do this with strangers. At this age too, friends are more than just familiar children of the same age; they are particular people who gravitate towards each other and may have special play routines that they repeat over and over again. Friendships are about negotiation and control too, 'If you don't do X, I won't be your friend any more.'

So even in pre-school children, friendships are important and useful. Research has shown that pre-school children engage in more complex levels of pretend play, are more effective at sharing and taking turns, and better able to resolve conflicts. As they get older, friends are better at solving conflicts, taking turns and sharing, and even better at solving academic problems. Older children who have good friends are more altruistic and have higher self-esteem than those who do not. Children who are not as well accepted at school, who do not have friends or who are very shy are more likely to drop out of school early.

It is therefore important that your child has regular playtimes with one or two other children. Perhaps once a week you could arrange for a friend to come over for a couple of hours. This will be better for her than going to lots of organized activities outside the home.

It will also help your child to settle at nursery if she can make friends with one or two children before she starts. Ask the staff which children will be joining at the same time, and invite one or two of these new children round to play. As mentioned above, it will help if you can 'scaffold' any interactions – set up scenarios for them to play, encourage games that involve playing together, intervene when necessary to help it all run smoothly.

How do children become friends?

Longitudinal studies have tracked the process children go through in making friends. When doing this, children need to achieve 'interpersonal co-ordination' and they do this when they are young, through play. So pre-school children who are making friends, develop their play into routines that demand greater levels of understanding and reciprocity. The highest level of this is fantasy play (see Chapter 15), which requires the children to be continually monitoring each other, to be clearly communicating with each other, and to be involved wholeheartedly. They also need to be willing to compromise. Fantasy play involves a lot of give and take. 'Let's pretend we are in a battle – you be the king and I'll be the dragon', 'yes, and let's pretend you were injured and I had to rescue you' and so on.

Researchers believe that this type of fantasy play helps children learn to manage their emotional arousal. While there are disputes, friends are more willing to drop their own agendas, to resolve differences. They agree more, 'I'm putting dolly to bed', 'me too'. There are more 'let's' and 'we' expressions in play between friends.

As children get older, forming friendships is no longer based in fantasy play, but starts to involve comparing skills and experiences, sharing gossip, exploring differences in taste and interests. But for pre-school children, fantasy play is the way to making a best friend.

What makes a child popular?

Young children who have a reciprocal best friend are much less likely to be excluded by their peer group. It seems that children without friends may lack social skills because they don't know how to join in appropriately.

Having a good friend or friends tends to enhance a child's social status in her peer group, but popularity or lack of it is more to do with how others rate her. It is interesting that what makes a child popular or unpopular is to do with her level of social skills.

In one experiment, researchers set up a room so that one child had to join the ongoing play of two other children. What they found was that the popular children didn't attempt to disrupt the play, but were sensitive to what was going on. Rather than trying to draw attention to themselves, they gradually joined in by making sensitive and appropriate comments on what the other two children were doing. They joined in with the current activity contributing in a positive way; this meant that these children were paying attention to what was going on and attempting to understand the frame of reference of the other children and were willing to adopt that themselves.

There were children, however, who always stayed at the waiting and watching stage, and these children tended to be those who were isolated, while another group, who were rejected by their peers, tried to join in by interrupting and creating a disruption.

Popular children are seen as leaders in groups, but in fact the leadership is more to do with being socially adept. They tend to be co-operative and skilled and good at imaginative play. In general, children who are skilled at imaginative play are more likeable than those who are not (see Chapter 15 for more on encouraging your child to be skilled at imaginative play).

Children who are not popular or who are rejected by their peer group are avoided. They then attempt to get attention often by intrusive means, trying to break into a group, which means they are more likely to be rejected again. Not having the opportunity to play with others unfortunately means that they have less opportunity to practise, so they become less skilled, which feeds into the unpopularity.

Children who are rejected by their peer groups tend to be either aggressive, or submissive (shy) – some of the aggressive ones also have lower cognitive abilities.

Although it might seem that breaking into small groups is a fairly natural and easy thing to do, some children will find this difficult, and therefore it is worth you modelling this for your child.

When you arrive at toddler group together, talk about where you might like to play, and who you might like to play with. Walk together to that group and show your child how to join in effectively, 'Can we play your game with you? It looks like fun! Can you tell us what we need to do?'

After a few times showing your child what to do, encourage her to do the asking, and then eventually you can progress to sitting on the sidelines watching and encouraging her to do it for herself.

Case history: Helen and Kathy

Helen has a lovely childminder, Alison; her daughter Kathy aged two adores her. However, Alison has taken on another charge to look after at the same time. Although Jamie is younger than Kathy, he is very rough and aggressive, and he often hits and scratches her; when Helen collects her she has marks on her. Alison is really embarrassed about it and keeps them apart in the house, but when she puts them into the double buggy he does his worst. Helen doesn't want to take Kathy away as the arrangement is fine in every other way, but it does worry her.

Answer: What a difficult situation! Alison knows this is a problem and while Helen can let her know she feels supportive, Helen must make it clear that ultimately Alison has to stop Jamie attacking Kathy. His behaviour is unacceptable and every time she lets this happen, he gets the wrong message. She will have to lay down strict boundaries with him, and physically restrain him from attacking Kathy.

Bullying

Having a good friend also helps protect children against bullying. But what about becoming a bully? Although most bullying is actually verbal rather than physical, there is evidence that aggressive behaviour if left unchecked will continue or get worse. Early lack of control (emotional reactivity, restlessness and short attention span) is correlated with later problems like aggression. Children who have a poor home life are more likely to be bullies; a home with irritable and ineffective discipline, poor parental monitoring of activities, lack of parental warmth, as well as experiencing aggressive means of solving problems at home.

Many young children can show aggressive behaviours such as snatching or verbal put downs. Some of these children will desist as they get older, but boys are more likely to continue than girls and aggressive boys tend to stay aggressive between the ages of two and five even though the overall level of physical aggression declines. Without intervention, they can later be delinquent.

This is why it is important to intervene when your child is not playing nicely. Even from an early age, you need to make it very clear what sort of behaviour is acceptable and what is not.

What to do if your child is being bullied

It is extremely important that you intervene if you suspect your child is being bullied. No child can cope with this on their own; knowing that you are on their side and take them seriously is extremely important. If the bullying is happening at nursery then you must involve the staff, get them to tell you exactly what they are going to do to stop the behaviour. If nasty behaviour is happening when you are there – for instance at a toddler group – then firstly you must protect your child, and then if possible, get the parent of the other child to intervene. While you cannot discipline someone else's child, you can ask that they do something. It will also really help your child if you comment on what is going on, for example, 'Isn't he being horrible? We don't behave like that do we? No, it is really not nice.'

There will inevitably be conflicts with other children. You must insist, from the start, that your toddler does not try to injure other children, removing and isolating her if she attempts to do so. Encourage sharing and taking turns – distract her if necessary onto another toy to help her let go.

If another child at the toddler group is aggressive, you need to give the right message to your own child. While you can't really tell someone else's child off, you need to let your toddler know that you didn't think that was acceptable. Tell your child that you didn't like the other child's behaviour and show her you feel aggrieved. She will cope far better, and accept your standards if you show that you know how she feels and are on her side.

Summary of this chapter

- Even from a very early age, toddlers are interested in other children and want to interact with them.
- Making friends is not as easy as it seems for some children. They need to develop several skills: how to break into a group without disruption and how to initiate and maintain interactions. Being good at imaginative play will help your child make friends too.
- Having friends is extremely important for your child's development, so you need to make sure this is happening and help out if it is not.

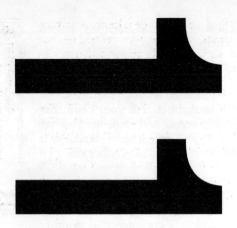

1
the difference between boys and girls

In this chapter you will learn:
- whether boys and girls are born or made
- what the real differences are between boys and girls
- about the effect you have on your child's sense of gender identity
- how you can even out the differences.

There is perhaps no other field of child development which sparks more debate than whether boys are born to be boys, or whether we make them that way. As with all such debates of course, the answer lies somewhere in between.

If we look at societies throughout the world, in general boys seem to be more predisposed to be physically active and interested in rough and tumble play, whereas girls are more interested in social and nurturing type play, and this is probably hormonal and inborn. Having said that, societies also reinforce that behaviour; in traditional societies where male strength is important for hunting or herding, sex role stereotyping is stronger than in societies which are made up of small social groups where tasks are shared.

Are boys more aggressive?

On average boys will be more aggressive than girls, probably because they have generally higher testosterone levels than girls. You will probably have become aware of this difference already as by two years of age, when they begin to play together, groups of boys will be noticeably more boisterous and aggressive than groups of girls. Boys are not only more physically aggressive but also more verbally aggressive – they use more taunts and insults.

You might think that perhaps boys are taught to be aggressive, while girls have their natural aggression 'suppressed'. However, if this were true, we would expect girls to 'let out' this suppressed aggression in safe, fantasy games, but this doesn't happen. Parents discourage aggression in both sexes, so they are not subtly teaching boys that aggression is OK.

Even if boys are naturally more aggressive than girls, in today's society, being over-aggressive is socially unacceptable, and you should discourage it in your sons and daughters equally.

Are girls better with babies?

Although we think that girls prefer dolls, in fact there is little difference between boys and girls in their desire to nurture. Your toddler, whether boy or girl, will enjoy feeding, bathing and nursing baby dolls. As boys grow older, playing with dolls becomes taboo, yet when children listen to a tape of a crying baby, although girls show more concern, their 'concealed responses' (their blood pressure, heart beat etc.), are the same – they both find a crying baby stressful.

A woman's pupils dilate at the sight of baby, but a man's pupils only do the same if they are fathers. However, men and women are just as good at handling babies and men naturally adopt 'motherese' (see Chapter 19), raising their voices higher like women to speak to babies. Men who bring up children on their own tend to adopt a 'motherly' style. All this means that men and women are just as good as each other at bringing up children, and there is no reason not to buy baby dolls for boys too.

How differences develop

The important thing to remember in all gender research is that the findings are about tendencies. For instance, even though it is true to say that on average boys will tend to be more aggressive than girls, an individual girl can be far more aggressive than an individual boy.

For the first two years of life, the similarities between boys and girls actually far outweigh the differences, it is not until they become mobile that the differences begin to become apparent. For instance, girls will tend to be more responsive to people, staying closer to adults; boys are more distressed by stressful situations which they cannot control, like separation.

Girls also seem to talk earlier, but then girls on the whole are slightly more advanced at all stages of development. For instance, girls usually gain bladder and bowel control earlier, they tend to read and write sooner, and are slightly better at arithmetic in the early years. Girls often do better at school than boys generally, although it could be argued that modern teaching practices suit girls better. Boys tend to have more learning-related problems; attention deficient disorder (ADD) and hyperactivity are more common in boys than girls, as is dyslexia, autism and certain language difficulties.

Case history: Heather and George

George has always been 'on the go'. He was a very active baby even in the womb, has never wanted to lie down or sit still, but as a baby preferred to be moving around, being held, and since he became mobile he has just wanted to race around as fast as he can. Heather always takes him out every day to let off steam, but she has noticed at toddler group his boisterousness is too much for some of the other children. He will run around, knocking their toys over, and he has also started throwing bricks around. Last week this resulted in another child being hit on the head.

Answer: children do have different energy levels, but Heather needs to channel this exuberance and attempt to control George a bit. He needs to start learning that running around is fine in some places but not in others, and he needs to grasp fairly quickly that hurting other children is completely unacceptable.

A naughty step is going to be a really excellent disciplinary method for George as he is going to really hate having to sit still, but it will be good for him to learn this self-control.

But Heather has to be fair to George and help him out here. A bit of letting off steam before toddler group would help; perhaps they should walk there rather than drive, or spend half an hour in the playground before he goes in.

Once at toddler group, Heather needs to really model quiet play and help George learn to do this. Sitting down together, they could construct towers out of bricks (which can then be exuberantly knocked over) for instance, or set up complicated train tracks so George can then enjoy pushing trains around.

Play choices

Under-twos are happy to play with the same toys, but again in toddlerhood you may see some sex differences in the toys your child chooses. Boys tend to prefer transportation toys, blocks and 'boisterous' activities involving gross motor skills such as throwing or kicking balls, or rough and tumbling, whereas girls tend to prefer dolls and dressing up or domestic play, but for many activities there does not seem to be a sex difference.

Interesting differences

- Research suggests that girls are more sensitive to smells, touch and sound, and more girls than boys can sing in tune.
- If you have a daughter, measure her height at 21 months, and double it. This will probably be a good guide to her height as a grown up. For your son, you need to wait until he is 24 months for him to be half his adult height.
- Boys on the whole have better visual–spatial skills, which includes being able to work out how an object in space would look from different perspectives, aiming at targets and map reading. These skills are useful for applied science and engineering.

How you reinforce sex roles

So some sex differences are probably inborn, particularly those which are hormonally influenced like aggression. However, the fact that differences become more marked over time, suggests that society is also playing a role in creating boys and girls.

Mothers at all stages tend to talk more about their feelings with daughters than with sons. By two years of age, girls are already responding to this by referring more often to how they feel than boys of the same age. Fathers tend to touch their newborn baby more if he is a son and may be especially attentive if he is the first-born, but may talk twice as much to their daughters than to their sons.

Both parents teach 'boys to be boys' by stimulating them to be active and outgoing, even discouraging many of their attempts at communication, while at the same time encouraging daughters to chatter. One researcher found that parents of three-year-olds used bigger words with their daughters and kept them talking longer even when the boys' language was just as sophisticated. They also found that mothers of pre-school children made more fuss over the appearance of a daughter, dressing her in more fussy clothes, fiddling with her hair, frequently commenting on her looks, and that fathers seem to prefer outdoor activities and physical play to intellectual play activities, especially with their sons.

By the time children are ready to start nursery, they have clear ideas about particular toys being meant for girls or boys, and that boys are more rigid in their stereotyping – nursery school girls happily play with boys' toys, but boys avoid girls' ones, even if they are shiny and new while the boys' toys are bashed and dilapidated. It is not surprising that boys are reluctant to be seen doing feminine things. People believe that it is far worse to be a 'sissy' than to be a 'tomboy'.

It is not as simple, though, as just having behaviour reinforced or copying adults, as nursery school teachers tend to reward feminine type behaviours in both sexes (quiet, sedentary activities near an adult) yet this does not prevent boys engaging more in noisy, rough and tumble play, even if this behaviour is discouraged. Also the children can't generally be imitating adult behaviour as they spend most of their waking hours surrounded by women, so what we must conclude is that children themselves are aware of their own sex early on and know which adults to observe and imitate. They must be picking up ideas about what is acceptable for boys and girls from the world around them, and of course there is probably also an innate predisposition to play and behave in certain ways.

What you can do to restore the gender balance

Although there are differences between the sexes, there is a great degree of overlap, and girls and boys are far more similar than we would expect, given how differently we raise them. We don't know why girls are better at language, and boys better at visual–spatial skills, but we do know that, with practice, the differences can shrink or disappear.

- You don't need to buy boys' toys for girls or vice versa. It is much better to use the toys your child already likes and to develop different skills and ways of playing.
- Girls' visual–spatial skills can be encouraged with shape sorters, stacking and nesting toys and lift out puzzle trays. Progress from here to Duplo and later Lego or Meccano. If your daughter prefers feminine toys, try the Duplo or Lego kits aimed at girls.
- Boys need to have their feminine profiles raised, so don't be afraid to encourage them to chatter, play with dolls, and to demonstrate a caring side to their nature. Getting a good balance between the masculine and feminine attributes for both boys and girls will help them grow into well-rounded adults.

- Boys have to find ways of behaving which allow them to be masculine without being aggressive. Help them work out ways to solve disputes using negotiation rather than aggression. You may well have to work harder with sons in developing communication and social skills.
- Boys need lots of opportunities to let off steam. Try to get out everyday and allow your son some time to run around. As he grows older, think about involving him in organized sports. Martial arts can offer a means of channelling aggressive tendencies in older boys.
- Do also make a special effort to teach your son gentle games which require quiet concentration.

Summary of this chapter

- There are some innate differences between boys and girls but these are also reinforced by society, and individual boys and girls will vary in the amount they conform to these expectations.
- Generally speaking, boys tend to be more aggressive than girls, but parents should try to minimize aggressive behaviour in all children.
- Boys and girls can be equally nurturing if given the opportunity.
- You can help your son or daughter to be more rounded by encouraging them to encompass traditional male and female behaviour.

part two

two

creative and
intellectual
development

12

the importance of play

In this chapter you will learn:
- that play is a vital part of your toddler's development
- why adults find it hard to play like children
- about the different types of play and their impact on development
- how play develops over time and what you can do to help.

Playing with your child should be the easiest thing in the world, yet many parents find it difficult. In this chapter we will see why play is so important for your toddler and what you can do to help.

Why is play important?

Almost from birth, children play. When a baby shakes a rattle or drops toys from her pram, she's not only having fun, she's learning about gravity, cause and effect, and if Mum picks up the toy over and over again, she learns about turn taking and communication. Adults also learn through activity; it would be impossible to learn to ride a bike by reading a book for instance, but for children, play is their main tool for learning the physical, social and intellectual skills they will need as adults.

The definition of play

Psychologists define play as something that is enjoyable, that does not necessarily have a definite goal or end result, that is spontaneous and voluntary – children choose to play and usually decide for themselves what to play – and that is active (unlike, for instance, watching TV or reading a book).

The ability to learn and to adapt to our surroundings makes human beings as a species extremely successful. Playful behaviour is part of this adaptive learning. Most intelligent species play; kittens and puppies play rough and tumble and pretend to capture balls of string, but insects, for instance, do not play. However, while kittens are simply practising skills they will need as adult cats, children's play is more complex and seems to have other functions too. Partly it is about modelling adult behaviour and thus learning about the world, but it is also about letting off steam and having fun, and imaginative play is vital for language and intellectual development. Play can also be 'cathartic'; children often express worries and work through problems or anxieties in their play, and indeed child therapists often use play in their diagnostic and therapeutic work. Play, for children, is as natural as breathing, and serves many functions.

- Play can be seen as an apprenticeship – your toddler uses it to practise tasks she will need as an adult, for instance, dressing herself or answering the phone.
- Play is like scientific research – it is about observing, exploring, speculating and making discoveries.
- Play can be used as therapy – sometimes your toddler uses play in a soothing or distracting way, sometimes she is simply avoiding being bored, but sometimes your toddler will act out a scenario, using play as a way of coming to terms with something unpleasant.
- Play can also be fun – it can be used simply to let off steam and to create enjoyment.

Case history: Julia and Benjamin

Benjamin is three and an only child. He is obsessed by Thomas the Tank Engine and his friends, and either likes to spend hours staring at DVDs of Thomas, or he carries various metal models of Thomas and his friends around the house. Julia feels a bit worried that this play seems quite limited, but when she has tried to involve him in a game of, say, pretend houses or to focus his attention on other toys, he doesn't seem interested.

Answer: While it is probably true that at age three, Benjamin should be more engaged in symbolic or imaginative play, it is usually fairly easy to steer a child in the right direction. Julia may need to coach him in this a bit, but it will probably work better if she works with what he is interested in. So she could involve Benjamin in creating play scenarios around his models. Maybe they could create an engine shed together where the trains go to sleep; she can discuss with him what they are thinking, and over time develop more imaginative scenarios. So start with putting the engines to bed in their shed, then may be talk about how they feel at night-time; and then discuss what they might do the next day, and then enact some scenarios – rescuing lost animals, delivering goods, etc.

She might also see if there are other children of a similar age who might come and play with Benjamin and get involved in these imaginative games.

Why is it hard to play when you are an adult?

The important thing about play is that it is spontaneous, voluntary, and meant to be fun, and it's for children. As an adult you are not driven to play in order to learn; you use abstract thought and reasoning. As we saw in Chapter 01, children's brains are more flexible; they are wiring up connections through experience. This means that they are open to new ideas and can happily accept that, temporarily, this broom is a sword or that cloth is a magic carpet, but we adults are more set in our ways, and this ability to fantasize with real objects has been lost to us. Our fantasies are only possible in our abstract thoughts.

In addition, children play at whatever takes their fancy at any particular time – that is what biology intends them to do. But if you sit down and say, 'Now I am going to play for ten minutes with my child' you are actually losing all that spontaneity, and thus play is going to feel artificial. Play is only going to work when you want to join in because it looks fun.

That is not to say you should not play with your child – your help is invaluable. But your help comes in steering play so that it is benefiting your child, rather than just joining in. Get involved when your child wants you to or seems to need help, guide her play if it seems to be stuck in certain areas, set up opportunities for play to happen and, finally, join in when you think it looks fun! You will soon be playing without realizing it.

Do mothers and fathers play differently?

Men tend to get involved with physical play more than women. Even a baby will quickly realize that Dad is a bit more exciting when it comes to rough and tumble play; he does bouncing games, makes lots of loud noises, and it's all slightly scary but very exhilarating. These games teach children a lot about physical boundaries and their own capabilities as well as how to interpret other people's signals; knowing when to stop for instance.

Mothers tend to prefer to play quieter games, making suggestions if their child seems stuck, but not interfering when it is going well. Interestingly, psychologists have discovered that mothers direct girls more than they do boys, while fathers are more likely to 'censor' their children, to be more critical of boys who play with girls' toys in particular.

It's worth trying to stretch yourself; fathers can have a go at quiet imaginative play, mums have a go at rough and tumble. No doubt there will be things you feel naturally inclined to do, but it is good for both yourself and your toddler to try new things. Go on, surprise yourself!

How play with other children develops

Babies and toddlers are very interested in children of the same age but, lacking in social skills, they are not able to initiate friendships or indeed maintain them (see Chapter 10). However, they do like to play with other children, and if you watch your child, you will see her move through stages depending on her social skills:

- Initially her play will be solitary.
- She will progress to spectator play; watching older children play without any attempt to join in.
- After some time spent in other children's company, you may see parallel play. Two or more children doing the same thing, side by side, but without any real interaction, for instance, several children might play in the sandpit next to each other.
- This moves into associative play; where they are doing things which relate to each other, close to other children, but with their own, self-generated ideas. There is not yet the discussion and interaction needed for the next stage. Here you might see several children playing in the kitchen; one serving food, one washing up and so on, but it will be fairly silent.
- Eventually they will work towards co-operative play, where play is all about interacting with someone else, and the play can now become richer and more imaginative.

You will be able to help your child move through these stages, by being explicit about what to do, and making suggestions. So when your toddler is engaged in parallel or associative play, you might want to say things like, 'See what Bethany is doing? Look she is making a cup of tea for her dolly. Shall we pass her some milk? Bethany, would your dolly like some milk?' or 'Tom is building a train set! Shall we help him? Tom, can we play with you? How about a tunnel? Perhaps we can make a station and you could make a tunnel?'

Helping your toddler develop play habits

During your child's first year, when she was a baby, most of her play was simply about manipulating objects and experiencing them through all the senses, and this carries on into the toddler years. She is asking herself, what does this feel like in my mouth? What happens when I do this? Pleasure in play comes from being able to control things, in making things happen.

You probably played with your baby all the time without even thinking about it. Changing her nappy, you might blow raspberries on her tummy. Pat-a-cake, round and round the garden; all of these familiar action rhymes may have become part of your repertoire. She loves these games because she is involved in directing the action. This verbal play is also teaching her the rhythms and turn taking of conversation.

Once your toddler begins to represent the world in an abstract way using words or mental pictures, she will begin to use 'symbolic' play. Symbolic play starts fairly simply – acting out everyday events like driving cars, shopping or housework, using toys and dolls. Children need fairly realistic props when they start, so what they play will partly depend on the toys you choose, and we will consider this in more detail in each chapter. Once she gets to about three years, if her language use is good, she will also become more skilled at abstract representation, her symbolic play becomes more elaborate and she will not need such realistic props. She will also get far more out of playing with her peers.

Providing for play

Encouraging play in your toddler is not about filling your house with expensive toys. In fact, the more expensive toys often work against play. The more flexible the object, the more your toddler will explore it, use it, and eventually let her imagination take flight. Unfortunately, there is a big trend towards electronic toys full of gizmos and computer chips, with scripted storylines and play ideas that are structured, and thus limited, by inbuilt electronics. Did you know that 80 per cent of toys now contain an electronic component? Toys that are spin offs from films or TV programmes can be among the worst, with limited opportunities for real play, and merely designed for instant gratification. When this is over, the toy has to be replaced with the next one in the series or more toys have to be bought to complete collections. The big players, who are after your disposable income, which is so much higher than your parents' disposable income was, have pushed many of the traditional high quality small toy manufacturers out of business. High rates of divorce, two full-time incomes and guilt about not spending enough time with children; all this equates to higher profits for toy manufacturers. So, shop wisely! Buy toys that your child might need to enhance her play, or make do with props from home.

Your toddler needs:

- time to play
- friends to play with (including you)
- resources (which do not need to be expensive).

Parents who encourage their children to play by taking it seriously, being excited about their discoveries, praising their achievements, being patient and encouraging, valuing the process of play and not always expecting a predictable end project, find that their children become more skilful players. Children whose parents discourage their play do actually limit the types of play they become involved in, which means, in effect, this limits their development.

It is a good idea to take your toddler to a playgroup and see which toys she is interested in, as there is likely to be a much bigger range of resources there. Given that the range of play materials you provide might be based on your own ideas about what is exciting and interesting, seeing how your child responds to toys you don't have at home, might give you ideas about what you might want to provide in the future.

How to get the most out of playing with your toddler

- Avoid feeling self-conscious – don't worry about what you are going to do to together, just make the time and see what happens. Let your child be the main instigator of events.
- Be spontaneous – if it is raining, go and jump in puddles, if it is sunny, go to the park. Or have a game of hide and seek indoors. The main thing is not to plan ahead too much.
- Make play a regular, natural part of your day. When cooking, allow more time so your toddler can help. Afterwards, keep empty boxes and packaging and have a gluing session before you chuck it all in the bin. If you are tidying up, involve your child and play at sorting things into boxes. If you are writing a shopping list, get your child to 'write' her own, and then when shopping, take turns to get things off the shelf. Spring clean your wardrobe and let your child dress up in all your cast-offs.

Summary of this chapter

- Play is not just mucking about, it is a vital tool for your toddler's development.
- You can do much to help your toddler's play develop.
- You don't have to be actively involved, but instead encourage your toddler by providing opportunities for play, and by helping her when she gets stuck.

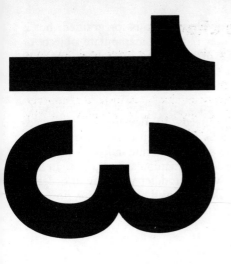

13

physical play

In this chapter you will learn:
- why your child needs physical activity
- what rough and tumble play is for
- how your toddler's play with objects develops.

To some extent we take our physical skills for granted, but if you watch a baby or toddler trying to manipulate objects or make his way around the world, you quickly realize just how much you had to learn in those early years, and most of that learning happens through play.

Your toddler is going to spend a great deal of time coming to terms with his body. He needs to develop balance, co-ordination, gross motor skills (how to use his arms and legs effectively to run, jump and so on) plus fine motor skills (using fingers and thumbs in order to manipulate objects). In this chapter we will look at how your toddler will play in order to practise and develop these skills, as well as suggesting how you might provide suitable opportunities for physical play.

Balance

We gain our sense of balance from our vestibular system, mostly relying on receptors in our inner ear to tell us if we are moving, stationary, the right way up or about to fall over, though our muscles and joints also contribute by giving us feedback on their movements. Most of the time we are unaware of using our vestibular system, but occasionally we become very aware; on a swing, in a boat, trying to cross a narrow beam. The vestibular system does not become fully mature until around age seven, and continues to develop beyond this well through puberty, and having vestibular stimulation helps it develop. This is why babies love being carried and rocked and why children adore playgrounds. It is surprising but true that learning difficulties such as dyslexia, Dyspraxia and Attention Deficit Hyperactivity Disorder (ADHD) are often linked to vestibular problems. So next time your toddler asks for just one more go on the swing, refuses to get off the climbing frame or roundabout, remind yourself that it might be good for his reading skills later on!

Gross motor skills

If you live a particularly sedentary life (and most of us in the West do) then it is easy to forget about running, jumping, skipping etc. as worthwhile activities in themselves, but your toddler really does need to develop his gross motor skills through activities like these. However, as adults we have become very fearful and perhaps over-protective of our children; worried about stranger danger we don't let our children run around outside without supervision. And if you have to sit and watch your toddler running around, then truthfully, you are going to limit the amount of time he gets to do this.

Unfortunately for you, it is important that you give your toddler free rein to run around and let off steam at least once a day, and I would suggest for at least an hour. If you resign yourself to that, then you just need to gear yourself up for it. Remind yourself that you are allowing him to develop balance and co-ordination, to develop his muscles and, with any luck, he will sleep more soundly for the exercise!

- The best place to let him run around is a play park, with swings, slides and so on. Take along a magazine or an iPod to give yourself something to do, but make sure you are able to see him at all times in case he gets into difficulty.

- If the weather is bad, many leisure centres have a soft play area which would do as a stand in or to give a bit of variety. Again take along something to do, or go with a friend so that you can combine your toddler's need to let off steam with your need for company.

- Take your toddler's sit-on toy to the park and let him whizz around the paths there. Combine this with a session feeding the ducks.

- Enrol in mother and toddler swimming lessons, or simply take your toddler to the leisure pool and let him splash around in the shallows or swim with you. Even better if there are slides he can wear himself out going up and down.

- Ball games are great for balance and co-ordination. Invest in a large soft football (not a real football which will hurt on impact) and take this to the park and kick it around with him. Initially he will run into it and be able to dribble it simply by pushing it along with his body, and by about two years he will lift his foot as if to kick it, but the co-ordination needed for kicking won't come till about three years of age, and catching a thrown ball will still be beyond him at this stage. For a bit of variety, let him use a large toy bat like a plastic cricket bat to push the ball around.

- If you have a garden, set up an obstacle race on a good day. A blanket to crawl under, crates to climb over, large cardboard boxes to hide in; ask a couple of his friends round and they can have races!

- In the summer there is nothing like a paddling pool for hours of enjoyment, but even jumping in and out of buckets of water will be equally enjoyable. Don't forget that toddlers can drown in a few inches of water so never leave them unsupervized.

- Ask at your local library or leisure centre for activities; you will be surprised how much is on offer for even tiny children.

- If you are really stuck then push back the furniture and let your child have a run around inside. You can have a game of 'chase the bubbles'; you stand in the corner and blow a stream of bubbles from one of those cheap bubble pots, and let your toddler burst them (incidentally when the pot is empty you can fill it with dilute washing up water). Or put on some lively music and dance around together.

The main point with physical play though, is that it is child-led, spontaneous, and to us adults may well look just like a waste of time, mucking about. Far better this mucking about though, than the pre-arranged, choreographed physical activity that takes placed in organized classes. Of course there is a place for these organized activities, and no doubt your toddler will enjoy these to a limited extent, but never let them replace spontaneous physical play.

Bikes and sit-on toys

It will be some time before your child is able to ride a bike; most children are well into their school years before they develop sufficient balance and co-ordination for this. Even using pedals will beyond most toddlers, though pre-schoolers usually can pedal a stable object like a trike or a bike with stabilizers.

Car boot sales and local newspapers are a good source for sit-on toys at this stage, and as roadworthiness is not so much of an issue, it is probably a reasonable place to shop. Look for a sturdy toy with good solid wheels where your toddler can place both feet on the floor to push himself along, and make sure it is easy for him to steer too. Check out whether you have a local toy library; these are great for supplying large sit-on toys for a limited period of time, which can be rotated to avoid boredom.

Fine motor skills

Your toddler develops fine motor skills through exploratory and manipulative play, which began very early on, when at three months old he started to play with his fingers and thus to develop hand–eye co-ordination. By the time he reaches his first birthday, he has already achieved one of the main abilities which sets us apart from the rest of the animal kingdom, the ability to use our opposable thumbs to grasp tiny objects in a pincer hold.

Bearing in mind that your toddler needs to explore and manipulate a variety of objects, try to provide a variety of things for him to play with. One way is to put a large box or chest of objects on the floor for him, each day, to unpack and examine, varying what is in it. Rather than having all his toys available all the time, put some away when he seems to have lost interest in them, and bring them out again in a few months' time. A small variety of toys which change over time is probably more interesting than an overwhelming stash of stuff.

Toys for exploration and manipulation

- Stacking objects like plastic cups which fit inside each other and when turned over can be stacked into a tower are a useful investment; these can also be used in sand and water play.
- Wooden jigsaw puzzles with lift-out pieces are excellent; your toddler will initially probably only manage to lift out the pieces and strew them around the room, but over time you can show him how to put them back, perhaps guiding his hand, and eventually he will master this difficult task. Conventional jigsaws will be beyond him until much later.
- A box of wooden bricks will be a good investment for years to come. Initially they can be used for stacking, banging, hiding and of course throwing, but later on they can be used in imaginative play to build walls, enclosures and so on.
- Supplement these conventional toys with everyday household objects: saucepans and wooden spoons, metal teaspoons and plastic bowls, biscuit tins, different fabrics such as silk, nylon, fur, wool, velvet or felt. Don't throw crinkly metallic wrapping paper and ribbons away, let them go in the toy box for a while.
- And of course once the toy box has been emptied, your toddler can climb in and pretend he is in a car!

Development of manipulative play

Age	Play with object	What it means
9 months	Brings it to mouth and explores it, then perhaps waves or bangs it around.	This random use of objects simply enhances play with body.
12 months	Investigates object first; looks at it, turns it around, then randomly mouths, bangs or waves it around.	Beginning to take notice of objects as independent entities.
15 months	Inspecting and investigating but now objects used more conventionally, for instance, pretends to drink from cup; hairbrush placed on hair.	Increasingly working out which action goes with which object.
21 months	Pairs objects – puts cup on saucer, looks for spoon to stir it with, gives doll drink etc.	Combining objects into functional relationships.
24 months	More involved play with objects; feeds doll realistically, puts it down for a nap after lunch.	Applying action patterns in sequence to form coherent whole patterns of behaviour.

Rough and tumble play

When your child starts mixing with other children, at nursery or playgroup for instance, he will start to encounter rough and tumble play; seeing other children (usually boys) rolling around together like puppies, play fighting.

While on the whole girls tend to prefer sedentary activities and boys tend to prefer this boisterous rough and tumble, neither will really join in until they are quite experienced. As we saw, initially children will just watch other children; this is in fact a form of exploratory play if you think about it – learning the rules of the game and also working out how to join in.

So initially your toddler will not join in with the play fighting, though boy toddlers will probably race about far more than girl toddlers, but eventually most children, and many baby animals, play at fighting and psychologists think this is normal and healthy. Animals rehearse behaviour they will need when they are independent; children find out about each other and their own limits. Rough and tumble play is not actually aggressive though it may look it. Children are working out safe boundaries, as well as letting off steam. You should only intervene when one or other child wants to stop but is unable. If your child seems overly fond of play fighting, you could widen it into imaginative play (see Chapter 15), for instance, suggest they play cops and robbers, or rescue teddy from the monster, rather than just killing each other!

Interestingly, even though rough and tumble appears to be something natural, done particularly by boys (and of course dads with babies), it is still a social activity and as such its development is probably shaped by early interactions with parents. Psychologists have noticed that first-born children watch rough and tumble more than later children who join in earlier on, which suggests that the rules of rough and tumble need to be learnt first, and so it is social and not aggressive. We think that play fighting might originate in physical play between parents and toddlers; tickling, throwing etc. Play fighting is common from age three right up to adolescence, and in all cultures there are recognized 'cues' so that children can work out this is pretend. However, for some children play fighting does turn into real fighting, and this may well be about misreading cues. So for your child to play rough and tumble safely he has to be good at reading social cues. If your child seems to be getting into fights, then watch him carefully and check that he is interacting well with his peers. (See Chapter 10 for more.)

Case history: Paula and Jo

Jo is three and mum Paula is at home full-time.

'He has always needed to be on the go, rushing about here and there. I've always had to make sure he has lots of time outdoors every day. He has also always preferred using his own imagination to something like drawing or playing with toys or really anything organized. When he was about two-and-a-half, he started playing at "being someone". It started as a policeman, and then for months we lived in Fireman Sam world; I was Station Officer Steel and his dad was Elvis. He has never really played with toys except as props – fireman's hats for instance. He is always on the go, physically and in his imagination; he rushes up and down the climbing frame which becomes a fire-station. Recently he has become Bob the Builder; he gets his tools out and hammers away. I have to phone up and ask him to fix something.

He never plays on his own – I have to be there, though he now prefers playing with other children. Older ones indulge him and let him boss them around, but with children of his own age, he co-operates more; they suggest ideas to each other, and have fantasy games that can last for half an hour.

He is not interested in drawing or writing; he can't sit still, so I suppose that could cause him a problem at school. He loves being read to, but that is at bedtime when he has wound down.'

Answer: Jo is a wonderful example of a highly skilled imaginative player (see Chapter 15), everything to hope for at this age. It is not surprising that he is a popular child, and that his language skills are highly developed. Paula has really helped him along by indulging in these games unself-consciously and by giving him the time and space to do what he was driven to do. As we can see, rushing about is not a waste of time; it leads to other important developmental achievements.

There is no need to worry about 'academic' achievements at three; social skills and imaginative play are far more important. We know he can concentrate when he is interested, as with the fantasy games. Writing can come later.

Three-year-olds need experience with other children, in and out of nursery. Try to arrange playtimes with one or two friends, providing toys for acting out fantasies, like dressing-up boxes. You may see play used to explore social situations and feelings. Doctors and nurses, for instance, is a 'safe' way to explore their own and other children's bodies. Beating up a baby doll is a safe way of resolving a conflict about a new baby, and doesn't need to be discouraged. Don't be worried about any rough and tumble play that appears – it is not actually aggressive though it may look it. Again the children are working out safe boundaries, as well as letting off steam. You should only intervene when one child wants to stop but is unable.

My child likes to play fighting games – is this ok?

Do war games create violent children? It is difficult to draw definite conclusions on this, but it seems that for children who are already disturbed or who have violent tendencies, sanctioning violent play can make matters worse. (See Chapter 16 for the influence of violence on TV.) Children who are difficult to manage do tend to also have more violent fantasies, poorer language and play skills, more anti-social behaviours and less empathic understanding. But we cannot be sure which is cause and which is effect, and there is no problem with a bit of exuberant play. If your son seems overly fond of fighting themes, it is better to work out where this is coming from and gently steer him into other types of play.

Summary of this chapter

- Your toddler needs to let off steam every day. Having time for spontaneous physical play enhances his gross motor skills and balance, all of which are important for later co-ordinating skills like reading and writing.
- You can help your child to develop fine motor skills by providing a variety of manipulative toys.
- Rough and tumble play is natural and is actually about interacting with other children – it is not a sign of aggression.
- However, if your child is struggling with play fighting, you may need to help with teaching social skills.

14

creative play

In this chapter you will learn:
- why creativity is important in children
- how to encourage your toddler's creative efforts
- how your child's drawing skills develop.

Many of us feel uncomfortable about encouraging creativity in our children. There is the imagined mess for instance; paint marks on the wall, sand on the floor; all that chaos for something your toddler might lose interest in after a few minutes. And then many of us had creativity squashed out of us at school when we were told that our picture was 'wrong' or 'no good'. Being creative can feel self-indulgent and pretentious, so why should we encourage it in our children?

In fact creative play serves several vital developmental functions at once. The manipulation involved develops your toddler's fine motor skills, whether this is grasping a pencil or kneading play dough to create something. There is also a sense of scientific exploration – what will happen if I do this? Play with paint, sand, glue and paper are all useful and valid, experimenting with the physical properties of different materials gives them ideas about form and construction.

Creating pictures or models involves your child in abstract representation, making something stand for something else, and in the grander scheme of things, it is also part of the initiation into our culture, where she learns about meaningful symbols and expression. Creativity involves the imagination and will encourage your child to become a divergent thinker; a person who is good at thinking of simple yet original solutions to problems. Creative people approach problems in novel ways. It is not about what they do, it's about the way they do it. Of course being creative is enjoyable in itself too! The opportunity to create something unique, to have control over a project from beginning to end, is tremendously satisfying.

Your role

Your reaction to your child's efforts will affect her creative play. Using slowed down videotapes, researchers noticed that young children were being directed in their painting by subtle positive and negative reactions from their mothers. So it is important that you encourage your child to be creative, and that you respond positively to her achievements.

Providing for creative play

Providing opportunities for creative play does probably mean time and effort on your part. For your own sanity, it is best to prepare an area of your house for messy work; kitchen or utility room for instance, or the garden if the weather is nice. A huge plastic sheet on the floor under the table and chairs is a good idea, and cover the table with an old blanket to protect the surface from spills; for small messes use a plastic cover on top.

- Start a collection of things like toilet rolls, cereal packets, old magazines, wrapping paper, fabric remnants, birthday and Christmas cards. You will also need to invest in some toddler-friendly glue – either a glue stick or, if you can face it, a bottle of runny glue. Pour a small amount into an old margarine lid and let your toddler apply it with an old brush. You can then throw it all away afterwards. You might want to invest in a selection of toddler scissors; wavy, zigzag and straight for instance, but make sure they actually have metal edges which will cut properly – some toddler scissors are made entirely of plastic or, so blunted they are useless! You might be better off using your own household scissors with careful supervision, as long as the ends are rounded. Spread some large sheets of paper on your table and have an afternoon cutting and sticking. Useful additions are glitter sticks, coloured pipe cleaners and bobbles; craft shops sell these sorts of things quite cheaply.

- Play dough is less messy than paint, and it is worth investing in a good collection of shape cutters and a decent rolling pin. You might be able to get adult cookie cutters and rolling pins from a junk shop. At first though, it is just a question of your toddler exploring the texture, so show her how to roll it into balls or sausages, give her lolly sticks and plastic spoons to stick into it and make marks or patterns.

Recipe for home-made play dough

- 2 cups of water
- 1 cup of salt
- 2 cups of flour
- 2 tablespoons of oil
- 2 teaspoons of cream of tartar
- 1 desert spoon of powder paint OR a few drops of food colouring.

Cook mixture over a medium heat, stirring all the time to prevent sticking. Remove from heat when mixture comes away from sides of pan. Knead and store in airtight container.

I found this mixture lasted for many months and was played with over and over again. When you take it out of storage the salt sometimes rises to the surface but disappears again when you knead it, and seems fine. Don't add too much food colouring as it will make it sticky. I found blue turned out green and red turned out pink, but my kids were happy with it!

- Sand and water play. Although ideally suited for outside, you can play with sand or water inside too. Water play can happen in a washing-up bowl or in the kitchen sink; surround the area with old towels or even newspapers which can be chucked out after they have served their function of soaking up the mess. Give your toddler various containers like jugs, cups and margarine pots to experiment with, as well as sieves and washing up brushes. Add a tiny drop of washing up liquid for extra fun. A funnel and toy water wheel are good investments

  You don't need a sandpit for sand play either. Some sand in a washing-up bowl or baby bath will work just as well. Use play sand, not builders' sand though. A big bag should cost only a few pounds and last for several months. Add a little water before use so it will mould into different shapes – you can use your play dough or cookie cutters (above) or the stacking pots (previous chapter), and of course spoons, small spades and the implements you use in water play. Right from the start, make it clear that sand must never be thrown.

  If you do have a sandpit outside, then have a really snug fitting lid to keep out cats and rain, and an extra brick on top will help prevent the wind from taking it off.

- Painting is a wonderful way for your toddler to experiment with creating colourful pictures. If your toddler responds well to painting opportunities at playgroup, you might consider doing this at home. Early on she will not cope with palates or mixing colours, and indeed using the brush will be a challenge enough. It is best to use runny paints, and to start with finger painting, or use a sponge. Once she is ready for brush work, put a centimetre of runny paint like poster paint in the bottom of a cottage cheese pot, sellotape the lid on, first making a wide hole in the lid, then stick the brush in this. Have a different pot for each colour. Use short thick brushes, one for each colour; small decorating brushes are good. A roll of wallpaper is cheap and absorbent and you can cut off pieces to size.

- Fat crayons are a less messy alternative to painting, but still need close supervision if you don't want new room decorations. Some crayons will double as paint sticks when dipped in water. Short fat stubby crayons are easier for toddlers to use and are less likely to break in their hands. **www.uptoten.com** has pictures you can print off for your toddler to colour in.

Being positive about your child's drawing

It is worth remembering that even the great artists had to practise. There is no such thing as someone who can't draw, in the same way as there is no such thing as someone who can't write, play an instrument, sing or read. All it takes is practice and positive reinforcement. Your child may not become the next Leonardo da Vinci, but she can learn to create a recognizable representation of something.

Be positive about her efforts, but don't use blanket praise all the time. Be specific about what you like and, if you want, you can make suggestions for improvement too. For instance:

'I like that lovely red, and what a lot of lines you have done! How about using another colour as well? I like yellow.'

Drawing well is about noticing things. You can encourage your child to be observant by asking questions such as 'How many fingers do you have?' while your child is drawing hands. Or asking, 'What colour is that dog? How could you make that colour with your paint box?'

If your child shows a real interest in painting and drawing, don't neglect art galleries as a good day out. Limit these expeditions to a very short tour of one or two pre-selected galleries though. The national gallery in London has a leaflet detailing a children's tour focusing on a small selection of paintings of particular interest to children. Modern art galleries like the Tate, with their wider definition of art, might well engage the creative toddler.

The development of pencil control

12 months	Grasps pencil in fist at top of shaft and will use both hands interchangeably.
15 months	Still grasping pencil in fist but holds it lower down the shaft. Makes dots and lines to and fro.
18–24 months	Increasing hand–eye co-ordination means bolder brushwork. Still grasping pencil in whole fist. May show preference for one hand, but continues to use either and sometimes both.
2–3 years	Now uses preferred hand (see Chapter 18) and picks up pencil or crayon between thumb and two fingers well down shaft. With this increased control she can scribble in circular movements.
3–4 years	More elaborate and diverse in colour, form and content and generally drawing people, houses, transport vehicles, flowers, animals etc. May provide running commentary about what she is drawing, changing her mind about what her picture represents as she goes along. It's not till she is over four that she announces beforehand what she's going to draw, suggesting that she has some idea in mind of what the picture will look like before she begins.

You can, of course, teach pencil control ahead of time, but don't push it so that your child becomes discouraged. You can also use your child's drawing to launch into writing too. Look for small squiggles (which are the basis of writing) and say oh look, that is an A for Apple, or O for Orange. Encourage her to write a 'shopping list' when you are going out. You can also help her writing by sharpening her perceptual skills in visual discrimination tasks; jigsaws, picture matching games etc., will all ultimately help her writing.

Case history: Ruth and Peter

Peter seems to like being creative, but Ruth really hates the mess. They live in a tiny flat and there just seems to be nowhere to do painting or the like. Also Peter will start painting or drawing or whatever, but then start running around the flat and Ruth is worried about him putting mucky hands on the wall. If she starts to clear it away, he comes back and insists he wants to carry on, but two seconds later he is off again.

Answer: There are several issues at play here. First, the sitting still and not running around – this is a discipline issue and Ruth needs to make clear rules and enforce them. Look at Chapter 02 for counting down to the naughty step – only in this case it would be counting down and then the paints are put away, no negotiation.

To help Peter contain himself it might be good to go out and do some physical play first. Perhaps an hour in the park will mean that he is then far more likely to want to sit still and do something quiet.

Second, creative play does not need to involve paints, which are probably the messiest option open to Ruth. Try paint crayons – like wax crayons – but if you dip them in water they act like paint. Or try play dough which is fun but less messy.

Third, it is useful to have a large box with a lifting lid into which you can put all the painting stuff and which can double up as a painting surface. Use old newspapers over the floor with plastic bags underneath these for spills, and afterwards the whole lot can be lifted and binned.

Summary of this chapter

- Creative play, whether painting and drawing, or messing about with sand and water, are all important for your toddler's intellectual development.
- Your attitude to your child's effort will either encourage or discourage her, so it is best to be positive but also make suggestions.
- Try to set up different opportunities for creativity – you don't need to spend a lot of money on this, but it will require time and effort in setting up and clearing away.

15

imaginative play

'Let's pretend': a favourite childhood phrase, which marks the beginning of an episode of fantasy or dramatic play between friends. The various types of imaginative play, fantasy, symbolic and dramatic, are incredibly important. Interestingly enough, imaginative play is actually primarily social, although we might picture it as solitary, and those who are skilled imaginative players tend to be the more popular children. Pretending to be someone else builds empathy, which is important in getting along with other people.

Psychologists also believe that the solitary symbolic play, which emerges at about age two (teddy's tea parties, pretend shopping etc.) is important for the development of language and abstract thinking. If your child is slow to speak, you could help him by showing him how to play in this way.

Some children have a natural disposition to prefer fantasy play, and these children enjoy play more, have better concentration and more self-control. They also tend to become better at divergent thinking, i.e. coming up with original and imaginative solutions to problems. Convergent thinkers tend to arrive at conventional solutions to problems, using logical and ordered thinking. We do all use both types of thinking, but most people have a tendency to use one style of thinking over the other, and the evidence suggests that if we are encouraged in fantasy play when young, we are more likely to use divergent thinking as adults.

Parents can influence children to become imaginative players by coaching toddlers to play at games like tea parties, and suggesting imaginative situations to pre-schoolers. Mothers who actually join in with symbolic play rather than just make suggestions have the biggest effect of all on their children's play. Children from deprived backgrounds are less likely to show any imaginative play, especially if their parents do not support it.

How imaginative play develops

Children's ability to play 'let's pretend' and to take on different roles and pretend to be different things doesn't really happen until about age three, and tends to disappear around adolescence, perhaps becoming private fantasy at this point. The very earliest that fantasy play will appear is at around 12–15 months, when your toddler might do something like 'pretend' to drive a car by making brmm brmm noises for instance. Early fantasy play will only be triggered by real objects or very realistic substitutes, and it won't be until about two years of age that he begins to use the objects to do things. Thus he can only use 'symbolic' or 'representational' play when he can represent the world in an abstract way, when he can think in symbols and use words to represent things (see Chapter 18).

Symbolic play starts fairly simply – for instance acting out everyday events like driving cars, shopping or housework, using toys and dolls. Children need fairly realistic props when they start, so what they play will partly depend on the toys you choose. As they get older and more skilled at abstract representation, symbolic play develops so that objects can stand in for other things, props become the launching pad for more elaborate scenarios, and so he will not need such realistic props – this is called 'decontextualization'.

Imaginative play with other children

Babies and toddlers do not need other children to engage in symbolic play, but they will enjoy adult input. You start your baby off on the path to imaginative play with imitation games and pretend games like peek-a-boo. With your toddler, you can initiate pretend games with teddies and dolls. 'Do you think teddy would like a biscuit too? You give him a biscuit! One bite for you, one for teddy.'

Most two-year-olds just 'parallel play'; they are happy to play beside other children, but without real interaction. They may accept taking turns, but mostly they view contemporaries as rivals for an adult's attention. So at this age your toddler will value your help in imaginative play. Watch your toddler playing, and without taking over or directing the play, just make some suggestions. So if he is playing with trains you could say, 'Do you think the trains would like to go to their shed now? Perhaps it is night time and the train driver needs to go to bed?' Just expand and elaborate on what he is already doing, making suggestions that involve imagining rather than just doing, as in the example above.

By the age of three, children mostly prefer to do their imaginative playing with their peers. Try to arrange playtimes with one or two friends, providing toys for acting out fantasies, like dressing-up boxes. You may see play used to explore social situations and feelings. Doctors and nurses, for instance, becomes a 'safe' way to explore their own and other children's bodies.

Shared imaginative play tends to come first; being able to play alone, developing into private fantasy comes later. By age four, expect fairly elaborate, prolonged but shared imaginative play. This type of play needs co-operation between playmates, so four-year-olds prefer to play with children they know, and start focusing on 'special' friends. By now, many treat adults merely as a 'resource' for answering questions, and prefer children's company.

How it works

The psychologist Vygotsky suggested that there are in fact rules of internal consistency in pretend play, that children implicitly understand these rules, and what might seem to us to be spontaneous make believe is actually chosen specifically and highlights the features of the world that are most relevant to the child at a given time. Some aspects of play are very realistic, but some are stereotyped in that they are created from the concepts the child has and not direct imitation. So household routines, like cooking or putting dolls to bed might be realistic, but fighting fires will probably be based on a concept and be less realistic.

You may notice your child 'marking' play episodes with a phrase like the universal, 'let's pretend' or something like, 'say that you are the policeman and I'm the baddie…' You may also notice that they adopt a special, fantasy tone of voice, for instance, gruff or whiny or whatever seems appropriate. It is as if they are announcing that 'now is make believe' by speaking in a modified voice.

Children often like to play at 'averting threat' – threat being fires, dragons, burglars, and so on – starting with identifying the threat and the danger it poses, defence and outcome. You can have fun spotting the process of this theme in your child's play. Depending on age, the ideas may need to be generated by toys – so a fireman's helmet might start averting the threat of fire, a sword the beginning of averting a monster threat, but as children become older and more imaginative, they will need less props, and a broom, for instance, could be a good sword substitute, a curtain will be a fire, and so on.

Psychologists use play therapy to help children deal with trauma, and sometimes parents are tempted to 'interpret' their children's play themes. However, normal children will freely mix fantasy and reality, will act out ideas that interest them, or recreate scenes from the TV without any deep meaning. Apart from this common 'averting threat' theme, other themes that children explore include being rejected, being ill, and empowerment, i.e. being helpless or being masterly. If your child returns over and over to a theme, or if his play does not seem to develop, this is more likely to indicate a problem than the actual content of the fantasy itself.

You will probably also notice gender differences in pretend play; girls tend to act out domestic scenes and, as these are familiar, they can be fairly elaborate. Boys may like to act out male roles, but will have less experience of seeing these in situ, and instead rely on books or the TV for ideas. Of course, although boys might be identifying with men, and girls with women, you are influencing them too by the toys you have chosen for them. Even though toddler girls will happily play with trucks and cars as much as toddler boys, examining homes reveals that boys are given far more vehicles to play with than girls.

Imaginary friends

Nearly a half of all children have some form of imaginary companion, especially between the ages of three to eight. (These 'friends' are usually gone by age ten.) Children who have imaginary friends tend to engage in a lot of sophisticated pretend play generally, and these are therefore a good sign, not an indication that your child is lonely for instance. Your child is not confused about what is imaginary and although he may make a good case for such a person existing, underneath it all he is aware they are different from real friends.

Case history: Amanda and Katie

Katie is four-and-a-half and about to start school. Her older brother Jack is seven, and her parents Amanda and Robert both work as computer consultants.

'Katie's favourite activities are what I would call "academic" stuff; she likes reading, and doing workbooks, probably because these are things I like doing. She doesn't really play on her own with toys or dolls, and doesn't play imaginative games. Jack will fabricate a long and complicated scenario with Playmobil; Katie will just set it all out so it looks nice, but then won't know what to do with it. She has always been adult focused, and for years didn't really want to play with other children. At long last she has reached a stage where she is genuinely social, and over the last few months has made a "best friend" at nursery. I am told they play marvellously together at Catriona's house or at nursery, but at our house, Katie tries to boss, and won't share. I think, being the youngest in our household, this is Katie's chance to have the upper hand. In fact she has empathy, and knows perfectly well what I am driving at when I try to get her to play nicely.'

Answer: Children are influenced by their parents. Katie's 'academic' focus is not surprising given both her parents have this background. However, developing her imaginative play could help her social development.

Popular children are those who are skilled and fluent at imaginative play. Shared imaginative play comes first; being able to play alone, developing private fantasy comes later. We can see these stages with Jack and Katie. By age four, expect fairly elaborate, prolonged but shared imaginative play. This type of play needs co-operation between playmates, which is why four-year-olds prefer to play with children they know, and start focusing on 'special' friends. By now, many treat adults merely as a 'resource' for answering questions, and prefer children's company. Despite this, arguments can be common. They understand the need for sharing and not being aggressive, but that doesn't mean it is easy for them. Perhaps Amanda could sort out with Katie, before Catriona arrives, which toys she will share, allowing her to put away a few 'precious' things. Setting up imaginative scenarios for the two to play at, like shops or camping adventures, will not only help the friendship, it could also develop Katie's imaginative play.

Summary of this chapter

- Parents can influence children to become imaginative players; coaching toddlers to play at games like tea parties, suggesting imaginative situations to pre-schoolers. Mothers who actually join in with symbolic play rather than just make suggestions have the biggest effect of all on their children's play.

- Try to provide a wide range of symbolic toys; cups and saucers, dolls or teddies, plus a good dressing-up box. You don't need to spend lots of money; a shoebox and tea towel make a great doll's bed, a big box can be a car or train. Go to car boot sales for old tents, old phones and cast off clothes for dressing up.

- Most play is based on home-life; this is what your child knows, so kitchens, bedrooms and bathrooms, driving cars or going shopping are favourites. Your child is using symbolic play to sort out his ideas about the world, and to develop 'internal scripts' which are really vital for language development. If your toddler is slow to speak, help him by suggesting simple scenarios like putting teddy to bed, or giving him his dinner, and do a running commentary on what you are both doing.

- As your toddler gets older and more skilled at playing, try to arrange playtimes with one or two friends, providing toys for acting out fantasies, like dressing-up boxes. You may need to encourage them to play together.

language play

In this chapter you will learn:
- how word play develops
- what reading does for your toddler, and how to get her into books
- about the role of TV and computers in your toddler's development.

In Chapter 19 we will look at how toddlers learn their native language. A big part of language acquisition comes through playing with words; singing, making up odd rhymes and jokes, creating nonsense. All of this is great fun, also very educational, and of course is social – telling jokes and communicating in wacky ways is only really funny when done with someone else. In this chapter we will look at how toddlers play with language, what the roles of books should be in play, as well as looking at the effects of TV and computers.

Playing with language and telling stories

In Chapter 19, we will look at language acquisition and pragmatics, meaning the knowledge of how to use language in a social context. One example of pragmatics is being able to tell stories, particularly well-known traditional stories. Before human beings developed paper and ink, and indeed in the days when reading was only understood by a small minority of the population, cultural information would be passed on from generation to generation by stories, songs and fables.

Being able to understand stories and tell them to others, or even create your own, involves several things. It involves understanding and using the rhythm of your native language. It also involves being able to move between your own and someone else's perspective. This ability to tell a story usually emerges at around age four to five, when children can retell personal experiences, but the skill in moving through different perspectives to tell a story with different events takes a while to develop, and usually children are much older, around nine, before they can really do this. A lot depends on how familiar they are with storytelling – and this is down to you.

Hearing narrative, for instance in being read a story, seems to help children to shape ideas, to explore lines of thought and to develop the ability to see the world from someone else's point of view. These are all tremendously useful skills, and so setting aside time to read with your child, encouraging them to create their own simple stories, and valuing these, is very important.

Experiments have found a link between how well children have interactive narratives with their mothers and their own control of their behaviour and emotions. Children who could tell stories coherently were rated as having fewer emotional and behavioural problems.

On a more fundamental level, the narratives we tell ourselves when awake or dreaming tend to structure our consciousness. Narratives are an important part of our sense of self. So for your toddler, taking part in storytelling, initially listening to new and familiar texts and then, eventually, creating them for herself, is part of becoming conscious; becoming human.

Toddlers and word play

Your toddler will love hearing rhyming, alliteration and rhythm. As she learns language, it becomes very satisfactory as well as great fun to distort language in this way. In addition, psychologists have found that being familiar with nursery rhymes and alliteration gives children a head start when it comes to learning to read and spell.

Rhymes your toddler might enjoy, which also have excellent rhythm:

- *Ring a ring a roses, a pocket full of posies, a-tissue, a-tissue, we all fall down!*
- *Round and round the garden, like a teddy bear, one step, two step, tickle under there!*

Invest in a traditional nursery rhyme book or look at **www.enchantedlearning.com**.

Alliteration:

The repetition of a leading vowel or consonant sound in a phrase.

- *Peter Piper picked a peck of pickled peppers.*
- *She sells seashells on the seashore.*

You could make up your own with your toddler.

Other word play:

- You may notice that your toddler often talks to herself before going to sleep or when waking up. She is practising the linguistic forms she is learning during the day.
- Around age two she will learn the conventional play noises like peep peep, ring ring, woof woof.
- After age three you might notice that she sings, hums or chants herself to sleep, or entertains herself with nonsense talk.
- Twins often develop private nonsense dialogues earlier than this.

- By age three or more she will use rhymes or riddle jokes, and by age four will enjoy word play that she can create herself.
- Pre-school children tend to teach each other silly rhymes and make up jokes together.

Books and your toddler

Your toddler will grow up to be entertained and informed by the internet, TV, DVDs, game consoles and far more besides. Perhaps books seem a bit dull, even irrelevant, in comparison. In fact books are still as important as ever.

During the early years, your toddler is at her most receptive. Establishing that books are interesting and entertaining is best done now, so that she's more likely to want to learn to read when she's older. And if you show your toddler how useful books are for acquiring information, she will understand that reading is a tool for research.

Early reading should not just be a solitary behaviour. Reading together can of course be a very calming, cuddly thing to do at bedtime, but use books during the day as well. You can work on projects together, using books to gather information. You can discuss books and use them to enhance activities and outings. Use stories as a springboard to speculation about how things could be different. Pause when reading and ask, for instance, 'How would it be if we had a tail like the dog in this story?'

Don't worry about following the text strictly; use it as suits you and your toddler. You will find as she get older, she constantly interrupts and asks questions, and this is fine. Books should be launching pads for ideas.

Using your local library

Libraries are a great, free resource that are vastly under-used. Most have a special children's section, away from the adults so there is no need to be hush, hush, where books are stored in large, easily accessible boxes, with child-friendly chairs or floor cushions nearby. Some libraries have regular sessions of storytelling or other activities. Use your library to the full, and when your toddler is older she will love to choose her own books. Any books that become favourites can go on the Christmas list, because the best books will be read over and over again.

What to look for in a book

Have some books which are for your toddler to use at will; these should be sturdy and non-precious, with good clear illustrations and very simple text or even no text at all. Bright, simple pictures, like Dick Bruna's for instance, are brilliant, and drawings are often better than photographs as the illustrator can leave out complicated detail, and create a better two-dimensional representation. These books should be easily accessible along with her other toys.

Then other more precious books can be brought out for reading together. First storylines need lots of repetition, understandable plots and minimal text. It's also useful if you enjoy the story too, as you will probably have to read it over and over again. One great early read is *Dear Zoo* by Rod Campbell (Puffin). *Apple Tree Farm* books, by Heather Amery and Stephen Cartwright (Usbourne), have a choice of storyline, simple or expanded, and a duck to find on every page too. Perhaps one of the best illustrators and writers ever is Eric Carle, and his classic *The Very Hungry Caterpillar* – though several other books of his are equally good – try *Brown Bear* or *Little Cloud* (Puffin books).

As your toddler grows, look out for books with good rhythm or rhyming text; this is useful for developing speech, particularly for a child who has language difficulties. There are old favourites like Dr Seuss books, for instance, *The Cat in the Hat* (but see also *Green Eggs and Ham* and Stan and Jan Berenstain's Bears book – *The Bear's Holiday, Bears in the Night, The Bike Lesson*) or try Lynley Dodd's excellent *Hairy Maclary* books (Puffin). Don't forget to teach your child nursery rhymes, which are not only part of our heritage, but introduce lunacy. After all, one of the great pleasures of reading is to expand the imagination and enter new worlds – nursery rhymes are the first stepping-stones to these. Progress on to Edward Lear's *The Owl and the Pussycat* (Walker Books) which combines poetry and creative writing madness.

Being aware of rhyming and alliteration really helps children to learn to read as they start to spot the common sounds in different words, and link these to the symbols on the page. This will also help with spelling later on. Learning to spell involves developing strategies, so if a child has got used to seeing what the word 'ball' looks like for instance, they can apply this to new words which look similar; 'hall', 'wall', 'call' etc.

Dyslexia

Dyslexia is a much misunderstood topic, with many people thinking it is simply about reading difficulties. In fact dyslexia covers a wide range of disorders, but tends to only come to light when children have difficulty learning to read. The traditional definition states: 'A disorder in children who, despite conventional classroom experience, fail to attain the language skills of reading, writing and spelling commensurate with their intellectual abilities.' See Chapter 22 for more on spotting dyslexia at this early stage.

Developing early reading skills in your toddler

- A child from a bookless home may find learning to read more difficult than a child who has handled and shared books from babyhood. Give your child her own bookcase or shelf where she can easily access books.
- Spend time playing word games and rhymes from an early age and when choosing books for your toddler, look for those which play on words using rhyme and alliteration.
- When your child becomes interested in books, create labels for things around the house and stick them up. Use lower-case lettering.
- When reading to your children, trace the words with your finger so she starts to realize that reading goes from left to right.
- 'I spy' and jigsaw puzzles are both good games to play with your child to develop reading skills.
- Take photos of events and play at sorting the pictures into the right order. Anything that involves sequencing is helpful as are games that need visual memory like 'Find the pairs'.

Television

It might seem that TV is a good thing as it is exposing children to language, and indeed at one point it was suggested to deaf parents that they leave the TV on to expose their hearing children to language. Unfortunately we now know that TV can't teach children to talk; for a start the language used is often too complex. Nowadays speech therapists even advise parents to limit TV viewing as children can learn to ignore speech as they concentrate on the visual. Learning to speak involves active, two-way communication, which is not possible with the TV. This is not to say that TV is a no-no, simply that watching it is a very passive experience, so try to limit the amount of time your toddler spends in front of it, and replace some TV time with reading.

Does TV influence behaviour?

When TV was first introduced, children in Britain watched about two hours a day. Now more time is spent watching TV than reading, sport, music and other leisure activities. TV is not all bad; some programmes with positive images and messages can be beneficial, for instance, programmes which have attempted to counter sexism, racism or prejudice against disability have been found to have some effect on children's attitudes.

Given that positive images can have a positive influence, what about negative images having a negative effect? What effect does violence, for instance, have on children?

Research is not as clear cut as we might think, because of course TV is part of general culture and it is therefore hard to carry out controlled studies. One study was done in the 1950s, when TVs were beginning to arrive in homes, and researchers were able to do 'before and after' comparisons. What they found was that children were most influenced by TV programmes if they were not put into perspective by anything in their immediate environment, and that the less intelligent the child, the greater the negative influence. Watching violence did not seem to increase aggression, though of course levels of violence were less then, and programmes were probably more conventional, reflecting middle-class values and attitudes.

A more recent study of two-year-olds who were exposed to violence on TV noticed that the toddlers responded with signs of distress and also increased aggression, and these effects were still noticeable a month later. It seems that for toddlers, these images arouse and release aggression not purge it. However, the effects were small, and we can probably conclude that aggression at home is far more devastating than fictitious aggression on TV.

Studies have also looked at sex-role stereotyping on TV and whether these affect children's attitudes. The conclusion was that there was little to suggest that the more TV children watched, the more sex-role stereotyped their views. The researchers concluded that children do not necessarily just passively receive everything they watch, but actively interpret programmes too. This ties in with the earlier finding about the more intelligent the less effect. Age too must have a role, as older children are probably more capable of critically questioning what they are watching.

It is impossible to really evaluate the effect of TV these days as it is impossible to separate out from other influences. Rather than worry about censoring each programme, what is probably the best strategy is firstly to limit the amount of time your child watches TV, because the more time spent watching, the less time spent in other activities. Secondly, choose age appropriate programmes where possible, remembering not to rely solely on the so-called 'watershed'. Finally, view TV as educational in so far as you can discuss as a family what you think of programmes, of issues raised and so on. TV will give you plenty to talk about, and can broaden the mind when you spend time critically evaluating it with your child.

One of the biggest problems with TV is that now, with so many more channels offering children's programmes around the clock and adding in to this the myriad of computer and internet games, children will have even less opportunity to let off steam. The result is that they can be mentally tired but have not used their bodies at all. This is a recipe for insomnia and bad moods. All children need some time each day being physically active. Some optometrists suggest that as screens dominate our lives, children are becoming more short-sighted. Screens, whether TV or computer, are fine in small doses, but try to limit the time they spend on these. Giving them, say, half an hour a day will encourage them to be more selective about what they watch.

If your child is really stuck on TV viewing, try to use it to develop imaginative play; for instance, you could play at pretending to be Postman Pat. It has to be said, however, that books have been found to be better tools for developing imaginative scenarios in older children.

Case history: Henry and Kathleen

Henry is two, the younger brother of Gemma (aged six) and Charlie (four-and-a-half). Mum, Kathleen, is at home full-time.

'Mostly, all three children play together at wild, imaginative games like lions and tigers, Robin Hood, pirates or whatever. Henry always joins in; I'm not sure how much he understands, he just copies what they're doing. The problem is that when they go over his head, he gets aggressive. Sometimes he misunderstands – they may be play fighting, but he will hit in earnest.

He loves to play with older children and, failing that, adults. He's not interested in children his own age. On his own, he sits for half an hour 'reading' – turning the pages and commenting on the pictures, or he watches videos. I know he watches them critically, because if the story is over his head, he wanders off. Some videos have enlarged his vocabulary; he repeats little phrases. He also likes singing and dancing along with the action.

Henry is boyish in that he copies Charlie, and likes cars. He particularly likes taking things apart, and likes contraptions. When he plays with cars and trains they tend to smash a lot. But he will also cuddle dolls, feed, bathe and tuck them into bed.'

Answer: Not being interested in his own age group is perfectly normal at this stage. Most two-year-olds just 'parallel play' – playing contentedly beside other children, but without real interaction. They may accept taking turns, but mostly they view contemporaries as rivals for an adult's attention.

Two-year-olds use 'symbolic play'; acting out everyday events like driving cars, shopping or housework, using toys and dolls. They need 'props' like teacups or shopping bags, so what they play will depend on the toys you choose. They are not yet capable of fantasy games, pretending to be someone, but older brothers and sisters may 'direct' them. Henry may be getting lost if Gemma and Charlie aren't telling him what to do, perhaps not bothering because they have each other.

Kathleen could encourage them to play together, as Henry will benefit. Research shows that while mothers do demonstrate everyday imaginative play using props like teacups, few mothers create wild scenarios like Charlie and Gemma.

TV and videos can be educational. If your child is joining in and responding, like Henry, it is a good sign. However, this level of involvement is hard work, and too much viewing could make him crabby. Limit viewing to no more than half an hour at a time, twice a day. Although TV offers some ideas for imaginative play, pretending to be Postman Pat for instance, books have been found to be better tools for developing imaginative scenarios in older children.

Computers, video games and internet usage

There is not yet much research on the effect of computers and the internet on children, but psychologists believe it will probably turn out to be similar to the research on TV. Some think that video and computer games may increase hand–eye co-ordination, but there are no studies to back this up yet. Some studies suggest that violent computer games may be linked with aggressive behaviour though it is hard to see whether children become violent through playing the games, or prefer these games because they have a disposition to be violent. In any case it makes sense to limit violent games as there are plenty of non-violent but exciting games on offer.

Some games appear quite addictive and parents have expressed a fear that their children might be socially isolated through spending too much time on these, but one study suggested that in fact playing the same games as your peers gives children something in common which helps them socialize. A few studies have suggested benefits in terms of relaxation and improvement of reading skills.

Summary of this chapter

- Word play helps your child's intellectual development in many ways, including assisting in social and emotional maturity.
- Books, rhymes and poems are part of our culture and should not just be saved for bedtime.
- Libraries are excellent resources and welcome even young toddlers.
- It is hard to assess the effect of TV on child development, but violent programmes may have an adverse effect on toddlers,

and too much TV may actually discourage your toddler from speaking, as well as limiting the time he has for more worthwhile activities, so it is probably best to limit TV viewing to no more than half an hour at a time, twice a day.

17

educating your toddler

In this chapter you will learn:
- how childcare might work for you and your toddler
- when and whether to send your toddler to nursery
- how to help your toddler settle into nursery
- what to think about when looking ahead to choosing schools.

By the time your baby reaches toddlerhood, you may be thinking about returning to work if you have not done so already. If you plan to stay at home, you may well be considering using a nursery or playgroup; you may even be thinking ahead to schooling. This chapter looks at the role of these outside organizations in your toddler's development.

Childcare choices for working parents

Parents have, of course, always worked, but only recently has our choice become either 'go to work' or 'look after children'. Our ancestors did both; working with children under foot while older siblings, aunties and grannies helped out. They would probably have thought it barbaric to separate mothers and children or to entrust our babies to strangers. However, few of us have a willing and able non-working granny or auntie living next door; even fewer of us have employers who would tolerate children under foot. So for most people the choice is stay at home, or employ people to look after the children. Employing outside help generally means a childminder, a nanny or a commercial day nursery.

Childminding

Childminding might seem on a par with babysitting, but in recent years the NCMA (National Childminding Association) has raised the standards of childminding in England and Wales with two quality assurance schemes, one for approved childminding networks – NCMA Children Come First – and one for individual childminders – NCMA Quality First (**www.ncma.org.uk**). SCMA in Scotland has similar schemes – see **www.childminding.org**. Childminders who work in these set-ups are fully trained and professional, most seeing their work as highly skilled and specialized.

The first place to start is to ask your local authority for the list of registered childminders in your area. These are people who are inspected by the local authority and all members of the household have to undergo police checks. Of course these safeguards will only go so far in ensuring that your toddler is going to be safe and well cared for; you should also seek recommendations from other parents and visit any potential childminder yourself, preferably while she is working so you can see how she interacts with the children in her care. Don't be put off by chaos, that's a good sign, though a dirty house may not be so good. An immaculately tidy house, however, is probably a worse sign still.

Draw up a list of questions to ask before you go; you might like to know what sort of regular activities she would do with your toddler, places she visits, meals and snacks she provides, how she will cater for your toddler's day-time naps. Ask how she deals with naughty and good behaviour in her charges. As your toddler is a guest in her house, her rules will have to apply, though if you have some particular requirements she will probably be able to accommodate these. Different routines and standards are actually a useful learning experience for your toddler, so try to go with the flow on this.

Case history: Liz, Sarah and Alex

In the past Liz has tried nannies, au pairs and a nursery but has now settled Alex with a childminder, while Sarah is at school.

'I had always believed a nanny or nursery would be better, as they are qualified, more formal. I now honestly believe that childminding is best. It is an ideal situation – I never imagined I would think that.

Childminding offers a home environment, and there is usually another child to play with. Alex is much more sociable than Sarah ever was; he benefits from his time with his childminder and her children. Sarah's nanny was shy and didn't want to go to toddler groups. We also had an au pair; domestically she was great, but she had little experience of children. She couldn't cope with Sarah answering her back, and Sarah picked up on her immaturity and said, "She's not a mummy, she's a child."

It is easier to judge a childminder than a whole nursery. My current childminder is a mother, which is another big advantage – I am less afraid of a mother than a nanny. I didn't know what I was supposed to ask, but my childminder was referred, and I went by instinct – which was proved right. How can you know? It is a fear; child basher is not written on their foreheads. Actually I was more fearful of the nursery, of institutionalized child abuse. Alex wasn't old enough to say, but he settled in really quickly at the childminder's. When I've occasionally had to use the local nursery, he hated it, he cries as I turned into the high street, "Me not want to stay at new school."

Like a builder, I would never use someone without a strong recommendation, and I feel the same about childcare.'

Nannies

Employing a nanny is expensive and is actually the least regulated option. Both day nurseries and childminders are regularly inspected, undergo police checks and have to fulfil certain hygiene and safety standards; anyone can call themselves a nanny and be given sole charge of a child.

While a recognized qualification is a good start, personal recommendations are important. Make sure any nanny you are thinking of employing has written references, and follow these up personally. Not only will this assure they are genuine, you may also find that people will tell you more than they are prepared to put on paper.

Remember that you will be this person's employer, so make sure you understand your legal and financial obligations. Get expert advice if need be, or delegate tax, national insurance and contracts to an outside agency.

Nannies either live in or live out; live in is usually cheaper, though of course you have to feed them and provide them with a good amount of completely private space. You will also need to think about how you feel about sharing your home 24/7; you may want to work out boundaries and house rules before you start. Make sure she can really be off duty when she is supposed to be.

As she is employed by you to look after your children in your house, you can be more demanding in terms of routines, meals, activities and the like than you could be with a childminder. Make sure your nanny is happy with what she will be asked to do, but also ask her opinion – she may have some good ideas of her own, and she will probably be happier if she feels she has autonomy.

Case history: Amanda, Jack and Katie

'I didn't fancy a nursery; I felt a small child would want to attach to one individual. I wanted someone my age with experience of children, rather than just a paper qualification. I was lucky that I had a friend who was a registered childminder. However, when Katie was born, she couldn't take her as well. It becomes more difficult to use a childminder when you have a child in nursery and a baby. The nanny agency found me Liz, who was in her late 30s, had her own school age children and wanted to work part-time. She is also live out, which means we don't get in each other's hair.

We respect and believe each other – you need a relationship based on trust. I don't worry about what is happening while I am away; I think it is less emotionally draining anyway, looking after other people's children.'

Day nurseries

In the UK almost 250,000 children under three currently attend a day nursery. This is a massive increase on previous rates, and to top that, the hours that these children spend in day nurseries has also increased, with some toddlers there up to ten hours, five days a week. This is partly because so many more parents work now, but it is also the result of government backing for day nurseries over other options.

Many day nurseries do offer wonderful opportunities for toddlers, with a huge variety of toys and equipment, as well as staff who know about child development and who will be working with the child's needs in mind. However, research also suggests that any benefits may be lost if children are spending long hours there; i.e. more than 20 hours a week.

Children under three need lots of one-to-one time with a limited number of adults, and some commercial day nurseries will struggle to offer this, especially if they experience high staff turnover. If a day nursery is the option you favour, then try to limit your toddler's hours to less than 20 a week, perhaps by flexible working or job sharing. Visit the day nursery during working hours (rather than at a specially arranged open day) and observe how the carers interact with the babies and children. It's easy to be impressed by expensive toys and equipment and ignore the quality of care. Find out about staff turnover and make sure that there will be a designated worker for your toddler. Ideally too, you want to meet this designated worker and see how she interacts with your child.

Pre-school education

School days may seem far away, but it is worth looking around now and beginning to think through your options. Remember that you will need to apply well in advance of start dates, and some schools have nurseries attached which would be an ideal way of introducing your toddler to his eventual peers. If your chosen school does not have a nursery, and even if your toddler is already experiencing outside childcare, it is worth thinking about letting him experience some other form of pre-school education, to allow him to socialize and to get used to the structure he will encounter when he starts school. Of course, if you have opted for a commercial day nursery as childcare while working, your toddler is already experiencing a similar environment to school. The other popular option is a pre-school playgroup. Catering usually for two-and-a-half year olds up to school age children, these are usually fairly cheap, and are often run by parents plus trained staff in a local hall. Like all educational provision, it has to be regularly inspected and approved by the local authority.

Is pre-school education essential?

More children than ever before attend a nursery or playgroup, although there is no legal obligation to start education before age five. It can feel hard sending 'your baby' to pre-school, but if all his friends are going, it's difficult to resist.

Studies have found that for three- to five-year-olds, pre-school experience helps children learn, especially if they are from a disadvantaged background (though as already discussed, the benefits peak at 20 hours a week and there's no extra benefit in attending nursery full-time).

However, these advantages did not last in the long run unless the child's home environment was particularly lacking. Children who were at home full-time were quickly able to catch up on the intellectual skills once they started school.

Your toddler's most important need is to develop social skills rather than to receive education as such. When looking at what's available locally, consider the environment which will suit your child best. Visit a few facilities while they are in session. Observe whether the children seem happy; how staff help quiet ones join in and noisy ones calm down. Look at the ratio of children to teacher; eight-to-one is usual. Take along a list of things to check, for instance:

- Does your toddler need lots of structure, or would he prefer more free play?
- Is he OK in a noisy environment, or is it important you select one that is quietly busy?

- How do the staff handle rough behaviour? How do they feel about discipline?
- Which primary school do the children move onto?
- Do they have enough space, especially for active children? Is there an outside play area with lots of equipment? Children of this age find waiting their turn hard, so if there is only one sit-on car, it could be a disaster.

Most important of all, go on your gut feeling.

Settling into nursery/playgroup

Often the children who find it hardest to adjust initially are those who are not used to a structured day. So a good first step is to get your lives into a routine, if you don't already have one. Settling at nursery is also much easier for the child who can cope with practicalities. For instance, although your child is potty trained, can he use a toilet on his own, wipe his bottom, pull up his pants and wash his hands afterwards? He won't be able to dress himself yet, but perhaps he could master an easy to fasten coat. Blowing his own nose and recognizing his name printed in lower case, are also useful skills.

As the big day looms, get ready by reading books or playing pretend games. Take teddy to playgroup, give him some lovely things to do, and then collect him at the end of the session with lots of hugs and kisses. The odd coincidental drive past the building will also get him used to the idea. If you know some of his classmates and their mothers, why not invite them round for a play? Familiar faces on the day may help him settle.

The first day

Be clear in your own mind before you get there whether you are going to stay as long as he needs to settle. Check out your ideas with the staff beforehand, although ultimately it is your decision. When you arrive, concentrate on practicalities. Show him where the toilet is and encourage him to go beforehand. Bring a bag of spare clothes even if it is months since he had an accident, and quietly give it to a member of staff.

Saying goodbye

Some children will go straight in without any qualms, but most will be shy or afraid at first, just like adults in a new social situation. Between 18 months and three years is often a clingy age, especially for children who are not used to being left. Do go at his pace; let it be his choice to join in. When you decide to go, don't say, 'I'll be back very soon' as he could interpret this as being in under two minutes. Say instead something like 'I am going to the shops now and I will be back after that.' Talk about it positively, for example 'and Mummy will get a delicious lunch ready for you when you finish.' However, you do need to say goodbye so he won't feel deserted. And never be late picking him up afterwards.

If this is the first time you have been apart and you think you will find it difficult, plan out a real treat for yourself on the first morning. Remind yourself that your child will be gaining a lot from relating to different people. Having time away is good for you too – many mothers think they are better parents for a break.

His reaction afterwards

A scream of joy doesn't mean he has had a terrible time; on the contrary it means he's been happy while you were away, but is also happy to see you. If he ignores you completely, he could be punishing you for leaving. Don't react in the same way – instead, wait (nonchalantly if you can!) for him to be ready, and give him a big welcome even if it is not reciprocated.

Sudden tears are common, especially for a child who is new to being left. He is simply overwhelmed with relief at seeing you and he needs lots of reassurance and cuddles. Try to exit on a positive note, emphasizing the good things that have happened: 'Oh look you've been painting. You can come again tomorrow and do some more, and Mummy will pick you up again afterwards, just like she promised.'

Settling in

Some mothers find that their child seems to settle well initially, but as the days pass, there are more tears and complaints about being left. Try to continue the drop off and pick up routine as normal. Don't start trying to sneak out without saying goodbye, for instance. Keep calm if he cries – he needs to know you can cope with his fears and anxieties. Sometimes it can be better to just say goodbye quickly and firmly, and then go. This seems hard, but if you linger, he may think that enough noise will make you stay. If this is the right strategy, the noise and tears will stop the minute you are out of sight.

Sometimes it helps if another trusted adult takes him, so that you can say goodbye to each other at your doorstep. He is then leaving you to go somewhere exciting, rather than you abandoning him. Some children remain unsettled until they have established their own friendships. You can help this process by asking him to invite a friend home to play.

Dealing with worries

While it may feel distressing for you, his anxiety is a perfectly normal reaction in the early days, and most children do settle eventually. It is important that you work with the nursery for solutions – make an appointment to discuss your worries. It is no use trying to squeeze in a discussion at the beginning or end of a session.

How to decide if your toddler is not really ready

Trust your instincts – you know your child best. It may be that right now is not the best time for your child to be coping with nursery – not all children are ready at the same age. But do listen to what the staff have to say. Give you and your child a deadline before you make the decision to stop going. In the meantime, look out for more worrying symptoms of anxiety – wetting or soiling himself, for instance. Perhaps there is change at home that makes the burden of settling at nursery just too much. It is not a good idea to start nursery when a new baby is due, for instance.

Find a way of observing him, unseen, half-way through the session. If he is obviously unhappy, refusing to join in, then it may well be time to worry. Perhaps if you could stay with him for a couple of sessions, your presence will give him the courage to join in to the extent that he can eventually let you go.

Remember, there is no shame if you decide he is not quite ready yet. You could leave it for the rest of the term and try again later. Use the time to leave him for short periods with other people; grandparents for instance. Mother and Toddler sessions will give him a chance to mix with other children, and to model nursery behaviour while you are still there reassuringly in the background. Perhaps you could also visit some other nurseries to confirm in your own mind that you made the right choice in the first place.

Thinking ahead to school

What do you look for in the perfect school? Would it be top of the exam league tables and have an excellent OFSTED report? While these are good signs, critics say that targets and league tables make teachers focus on the wrong things, so that some good schools are simply those who can outmanoeuvre the assessment system. As with day nursery, look at atmosphere, facilities, how the staff and children interact. Ask friends for recommendations. But try to use your local school if you can. A distant school would need to be really exceptional for you to accept long commutes, and remember that your child will want local friends as he grows older. The further the school, the more of a taxi service you will become.

Summary of this chapter

- Nowadays most parents of pre-school children work. Selecting childcare can feel like negotiating a minefield, so look at all your options carefully.
- Some pre-school experience is useful but only if your toddler is ready.
- Think ahead to school, but try to choose one as local as possible; in the long run your child will thank you for this.

part

three

cognitive development

18

the development of knowledge

In this chapter you will learn:
- how your toddler builds up a body of knowledge
- how your toddler's thinking processes develop
- whether thought creates language or language creates thought.

Experience is continually rewiring our brains. Active synapses and pathways are strengthened and inactive ones weakened according to the sights, sounds, feelings and events of daily life. For your toddler, the repeated stimulation that occurs during learning a new skill, experiencing the same type of event over and over, primes her neurons to respond more sensitively in the future. Learning, then, is really just a manifestation of the ability of each person's brain to modify itself according to his or her unique experiences.

Your toddler's brain becomes specialized

Initially your toddler is focusing on the here and now, on what she is experiencing moment by moment through her senses, but through time the growth in the number of associations between neurons for different objects, people and events gradually leads to the linking of certain common features and hence to the eventual development of more abstract and general ideas.

As the brain makes links, it is gradually specializing, becoming expert at whatever your toddler's environment requires of her. If she plays a lot of sport, she will become more athletic. If she comes from a musical family, where music is listened to and played continually, she will develop musical skills. We know that musicality is not something located in any specific area of the brain, but that early experience primes the brain in general to notice musical patterns. It is harder to learn instruments after the age of ten, for instance, and perfect pitch is usually only found in those who took up music before the age of seven.

Children's brains take a long time to develop – parts of the brain, such as those responsible for self-control, are not fully mature until late adolescence. Brain imaging studies of children have shown that, until they are about six years of age, grammar is processed by both hemispheres of the brain, and that it is only after this that the left hemisphere specializes, but in children who have had their left hemisphere removed before this age (to treat epilepsy) the right hemisphere takes over and the children can still use language normally.

Will my toddler be left- or right-handed, and why?

Hand preference changes over the first two years of life. You may see your toddler swapping hands without thinking when she is scribbling, but this does not mean she is likely to be ambidextrous, it is just a reflection of the fact that handedness is generally unstable at this age and is often not fixed until late pre-school age.

Between 85 and 90 per cent of people are right-handed, though this percentage varies among different cultures. Genes are at least partly responsible, since left-handed parents are far likelier than right-handed parents to have left-handed children, but there is no simple genetic model that can account for the fact than only half of all children who have two left-handed parents will themselves be left-handed and that a child is likely to end up left-handed if her mother alone is left-handed as opposed to her father alone.

The other problem is in being sure about the real percentage of left-handers in the population. There are cultural influences; until only a couple of generations ago, left-handed children in the UK were encouraged to use their right hand, and there are still cultures where left-handedness is considered unacceptable, and in these places there are fewer left-handed people. However, when the children of the same ethnic origin are reared in Western countries the rates of left-handedness are higher.

Children also tend to copy those around them, which might explain why mothers are more likely to pass left-handedness on to their children. Ultimately though, handedness is reflected in the structure of the brain; right-handed adults have deeper fissures and a higher ratio of grey to white matter in the left than the right frontal lobe and the asymmetry between the hemispheres arises as early as 29 weeks of gestation in the language areas of the brain. But given how flexible brain development is, handedness is unlikely to create huge differences in personality or skills.

Case history: Linda and Steve

Linda is worried about Steve who is 14 months old and has still not said anything discernible. Her friends' children seem to have fairly large vocabularies now and some of them are even using short sentences. She is of the opinion that there is no race, but she is wondering if it is time to seek help.

Answer: most children would have uttered their first words by now, though parents don't always notice these. There is then sometimes a pause while the child's brain seems to consolidate before the next burst of language happens, but it is probably worth getting an outside opinion. Your health visitor is a good person to talk to at this stage. She can also refer you for a specialist hearing test. Even though Steve may appear to be hearing, some problems are not always obvious but do manifest themselves in late language development.

In the meantime there is a lot that Linda can to do help Steve. Firstly she should cut out any extraneous noise during the day – no background TV or radio, as children sometimes tune out listening if there is too much in the way of incomprehensible speech going on. Secondly she could really make an effort to talk to Steve slowly and clearly (see next chapter). Games like shape sorters, pairs, snap etc all help language interestingly enough, because they help develop abstract thinking. Linda should also spend time reading simple books with Steve (see Chapter 16 for recommendations).

How children organize their knowledge

It comes as no surprise to most adults that babies and toddlers love to learn, and they learn through being active in their environment. Initially, for the first year or two of life, your baby is experiencing the world through her senses, and making discoveries through what she sees, hears, smells and tastes, and through the effect of her body on the world around her. Everything is very much 'here and now' – she does not think about the future or reflect on the past as the mental processes that would enable her to do this are not yet developed. Over this period of time, through acting on the world with her body, she begins to understand cause and effect, and begins to develop 'internal mental representations', which will, in the future, allow abstract thought and language. We need internal mental representations to move outside the here and now and to think about things which are not there. For instance, in order for your baby to know that you exist when you are not there, she needs to have some sort of internal mental representation of you. Or to be able to speak, she has to have some understanding that the word, 'mummy' can represent you.

Creating mental representations

Children seem to build up knowledge by creating hypotheses and then testing these. For instance, your child might think, 'dogs are things with four legs', and seeing a dog or thinking about a dog fires off all the neural pathways that are created around this concept. But then they encounter cats, and discover that they are slightly different so the concept or hypothesis, if you like, becomes 'dogs are hairy things with four legs that bark, cats are furry things with four legs that miaow.' You can see that these two definitions are fairly similar and are probably linked in many ways in the brain, so if four legs comes to mind, cat and dog will be evoked, but also chair. Scientists can measure mental representations by asking people questions and measuring their response time. For instance, if you were asked, 'Is a duck a bird?' your response would be slightly slower than if you were asked, 'Is a robin a bird?' This is because a robin is a more 'prototypical' bird than a duck, and presumably the connections between robin and bird are stronger in your brain than the connections between duck and bird.

The relationship between language and thought

Which comes first, thought or language? That is a question which has fascinated psychologists for ages. Is language dependent on and does it arise out of your child's ability to form concepts? Or does her ability to think in abstract create the need for language?

Some psychologists believe that as a baby gets older and starts to identify different, specific objects and thus begins to identify categories, these internal representations of objects spark the need for words, so thought produces language. As their first words usually focus on family, actions or objects, you could argue that this shows that they are expressing aspects of their environment that they already understand non-verbally. There is some support for this viewpoint when we look at the cognitive abilities of deaf children, particularly those who were denied access to sign language, who are able to reason and solve problems even with limited language. Oliver Sacks describes Joseph, a deaf child reared without sign language for his first ten years. Apparently, Joseph could categorize objects, but could not hold abstract ideas in his head. He was very literal, stuck in the present. So we can think without language, but it limits us.

An example that psychologists might give of thought driving the need for language is that initially your toddler may use the word dog to apply to all animals, so when she sees a cat, she says 'dog'. Now as she needs to develop a different mental representation for cats, she recognizes that they can be distinguished from dogs, so she then acquires a new word to apply to cats. However, you could also argue that the child is not using the word dog to apply to cat because she lacks a mental concept of cat, but you might argue that she is instead using language in a creative way – to communicate.

And this view of thought preceding language does seem to ignore the role we parents play in teaching our children about the world, which we do mostly through talking. Could it be, therefore, that language drives thought, that parents talk to children and in response the children develop mental concepts as a result of hearing the words we use? If this were true then knowledge in any particular society might be culturally specific; memory, intelligence, reasoning – all would be influenced by culture. And indeed there is evidence that this is true. Cultural constructs like myths, fairy tales, songs and poems all form part of a shared cultural knowledge which children join. Anthropologists have discovered that skills are 'skewed' to suit different cultures, for instance, the Kpelle of Liberia are more skilled at estimating weights of rice than Americans, but less skilled at estimating length, because that is what their culture requires.

In English, nouns convey meaning, and English-speaking parents will spend a lot of time pointing to objects and giving them names, but in Korean, different verb endings convey different meanings, and Korean mothers will often miss out nouns in talking to their children, the result being that 18-month-old Korean children, not only use more verbs than

English speaking children of the same age, but they also learn how to solve problems using actions before English-speaking children, whereas English-speaking children start categorizing objects earlier, sorting objects into different piles, for instance.

In fact it is probably fair to say that there is an interaction; as we have seen children without language can think, on the other hand children's ways of thinking can be influenced by the language they use. As your toddler becomes acquainted with something, she needs to find a new word for the knowledge she is uncovering, and in the process the knowledge becomes easier to grasp and to communicate to others.

Language helps us to organize our thoughts, to remember and to plan and is arguably our species' most useful tool. Abstract thought, thinking about the past and future – all this seems to depend on language to a great extent, but it also requires memory. We will be looking both at how your child will acquire language, and also how her memory develops, in the following two chapters.

Summary of this chapter

- Your toddler will move gradually from understanding the world in the here and now through her senses and actions, to being capable of abstract thought and reasoning when she is older.
- The environment your toddler grows up in will shape the skills and knowledge she acquires.
- Language and thought seem to interact; your toddler will grasp a new concept through an interaction between hearing the name for it and experiencing the concept in the abstract.

19

understanding language

In this chapter you will learn:
- why it takes so long to learn to speak
- why toddlers make grammatical mistakes
- how you can help your toddler to communicate.

Language is the most useful tool we have as a species. We take it for granted that our children will learn to speak given time, but if you think about it, what they actually achieve in these early years of life is quite remarkable.

Why languages are so difficult to learn

Toddlers make it seem effortless, but just remember the hours you spent at school attempting to acquire a smattering of French and then, if you actually visited France, think of the struggle to grasp even the simplest phrase thrown at you despite these years of education.

The problem is that we do not speak, as we write, with gaps between words; instead we produce a continuous stream of sound, with all the words flowing together. It is our brain which breaks this continual sound wave down into single sounds, a task which is beyond even the most advanced computer at this point in time, but which toddlers can do after only a year of being immersed in this cacophony.

Furthermore, there is the problem that all voices produce different sound waves in making what should be the same sounds; any single word will vary depending on whether the person is male, female or child, how quickly they are speaking, and whether they are shouting or whispering. Voices sound different depending on accent, the shape of the mouth – so many thousands of possibilities, and our brain handles each and every one without any conscious effort.

The final problem is that even for the same person speaking in the same way, a small difference in sound can produce a huge difference in meaning. Think of run, sun, won and fun, or fair, fur, far etc.

Currently we can only get a computer to understand spoken English if we use very few and specific words, each separated by a pause, and even then it can only cope with one voice. By age three, in contrast, an English-speaking child can understand a language which contains over 75,000 words, spoken at normal speed by any number of different people.

How babies make sense of what they hear

So how do babies manage to make sense of continuous streams of sound so effortlessly, whereas we adults struggle with listening to foreign languages? It seems that babies are primed to learn language from incredibly early on. Whereas newborn babies struggle to see detail, they have fantastically acute hearing, and this is developing in utero; their sense of hearing emerging early on, being fully developed at around four-and-a half months' gestation, the sounds of voices travelling easily through the amniotic fluid. Babies in the womb respond to familiar music, and can recognize familiar stories as well as themes from soap operas. At birth, they prefer listening to what will be their native tongue over a foreign language, so they have already begun to tune into its peculiarities.

What they are doing is using this time in the uterus to tune into the sounds of their own language. Potentially they could speak any language; after all they could be born in any country and any culture, so initially they need to get used to their own sounds.

Tuning in

Imagine the recording of a sound wave that is human speech. On paper this will appear as a continuous wave, and due to the variations we discussed above, it is impossible to look at this piece of paper and say, 'there is an l or there is an r', yet we will be able to hear these sounds distinctly. If you then use a speech synthesizer to gradually change the sound 'r' to 'l', although the synthesizer produces a range of sounds, which you could see changing on the paper, you will actually only hear 'r, r, r...' suddenly changing to 'l, l, l...' Japanese people won't hear the change at all – they continue to hear the same sound.

What is happening is that each culture divides sounds into categories particular to them. We won't hear the shifts that Thai speakers hear for instance, while the Japanese don't use 'r' and 'l' and so can't hear them. But incredibly, babies can hear them all – Japanese babies hear the shift from 'r' to 'l', English-speaking babies will hear the shifts in Thai, even if they have never heard these sounds before. They are born without prejudice – they will listen to any human sound. However, somewhere between six and 12 months the ability to discriminate all these sounds goes, and from then on your baby only notices the sounds particular to his culture. By paying attention to the language of his culture, he stores a representation of the most typical 'r', most typical 'l' and so on, and somewhere between six and 12 months he has a store in his memory of culturally typical phonemes (the smallest units of perceptible speech). The repeated exposure to particular sounds reinforces certain categories and, if you like, deletes others, and thus your toddler develops 'prototypes' of sounds. Any sounds he hears after this period of time are compared to these prototypes and interpreted accordingly. This is why, despite the fact we **hear** (i.e. our ear will transmit the sound to our brain) hundreds of slightly different versions of 'd', we will **perceive** them all (i.e. interpret this sound) as one, prototypical 'd'.

Of course it is not just about distinguishing between English and other languages, there will be national, regional and local accents to develop. For instance, Scottish babies will be hearing the 'ch' ending to words like 'loch', which English children will eventually struggle to pronounce properly.

As well as tuning into the prototypical sounds of their own language, babies are paying attention to the rhythms of speech. By nine months, English-speaking babies have learnt that we emphasize the first syllable of every word (most other languages don't). They have also learnt which sound combinations are possible in their own languages and which are incorrect. By paying attention to the melody and rhythm of speech, they notice things like where the gaps before and after utterances should be.

This tuning in to the rhythm of speech is something your baby was driven to do, but he did not have to do it on his own. From birth you interacted with him, sang to him, tuned him in to rhythms through dancing with him or singing nursery rhymes to him. But more than this, you were also instinctively teaching him how to listen to the patterns of the English language.

'Motherese' – what parents do to help their children speak

When we come face to face with a baby – we all do it – we put on a silly voice. Sometimes you might feel a little self-conscious, thinking you sound daft to other adults. However, this silly voice is a powerful, innate mechanism which all human beings use in order to help children to speak.

Motherese is actually a misnomer, because all adults use it when faced with babies; mothers, fathers, even people without children. It is found in other cultures, and it works in a very specific way. Firstly the voice rises, as much as an octave or even higher, the pitch varies while talking so it is melodic or 'sing-songy', sentences are shorter and simpler, there is a lot of repetition, consonants are formed properly, vowels are exaggerated, so overall speech is slower and more distinct with proper pauses between words. Motherese uses concrete nouns and proper nouns, avoiding pronouns and conjunctions, and will usually refer to what is happening here and now. Most of those problems in distinguishing that continuous stream of sound are thus overcome; perhaps therefore on holiday abroad it might help if we were spoken to in Motherese!

Motherese seems to be a particularly effective tool in helping babies to focus on the words of their culture, and when babies are younger their mothers emphasize the vowels of their own language in exactly the right way to allow their babies to develop the right prototypes for their language.

So the really important message is that baby talk is not silly, it is a vital tool in helping your child learn to speak. Don't use daft vocabulary though, like broom broom for car or woofie for dog, as your toddler will only have to re-learn the names of things. It is fine to use euphemisms for body parts but call other things by their proper names. Motherese is more to do with the way you talk; slowly and distinctly, with a higher pitched voice and lots of repetition.

To give an example: in the early days you might have said: 'Hello there baby! Who's a lovely boy then! Aren't you a big boy!' etc. With your toddler you might say, 'Where are your shoes? Can you find your shoes? Shall we put them on? Can you do it all by yourself? Aren't you clever – you've found your shoes! Well done!'

What your toddler has to learn in order to communicate

To use language – to interpret what people say and also to respond in words, children need to learn four different things:

- the rules of sound (phonetics)
- the meaning of the sounds (semantics)

- grammar (syntax)
- knowledge of social context (pragmatics).

So as we have seen already, your toddler has to learn to distinguish (perceive) particular sound units called phonemes – the smallest meaningful units of language (phonetics). These meaningless but culturally specific sounds are combined into larger units called morphemes, such as the word ending '–ed' which means past tense (semantics).

He also has to understand meaning through word order or combination (syntax). So 'the boy bit the dog' has a different meaning from 'the dog bit the boy'. Finally, there is interpreting the meaning in context; knowing whether a speaker means bow or bough, horse or hoarse (pragmatics).

Babies do not learn language just through adults naming objects for them, which they then copy. This would not explain how they learn to talk about things they don't directly experience, or indeed how they learn to use verbs, adjectives or even prepositions and word endings, i.e. syntax. There is obviously some imitation happening, because children whose mothers talk to them more have larger vocabularies. But as children grow, they recombine words to create their own, unique sentences, even applying child-like rules of grammar: 'I hurted my head' – a child will not be imitating someone when he creates a sentence like this, though logically this should be grammatically correct.

Learning syntax

Syntax is perhaps the particular aspect of language which sets us apart from other animals. After all, animals make noises and communicate with each other – sometimes in a fairly sophisticated manner – but syntax allows us to take short cuts – to express complicated ideas with a relatively small number of noises, and to be precise about these ideas. It is syntax which allows us to plan ahead, to hypothesize, to imagine.

Interestingly too, like phonetics, syntax is harder to acquire the later you learn a language. Studies of immigrants show that they have two problems acquiring a new language as an adult: pronunciation (which is to do with that early learning of phonetics) and grammar. Researchers studying immigrants to the USA found that if they arrived before the age of seven they make few grammatical errors, but there is a steady rise in error rate as the immigrant was older on arrival, even after living in the USA for ten years.

Studies of deaf adults who had been signing for at least 30 years show similar results; those who were born to deaf parents and thus exposed to ASL (American Sign Language) from birth were found to have better grammar than those who started learning to sign when they entered a special school for deaf children at age four to six, whereas those who had joined the school after the age of 12 consistently signed in ungrammatical ways, despite the fact that they had now been signing for over 20 years.

Right from the point at which children start to string words together, they do it grammatically, and while they may be copying their parents, they are also creating their own grammatically correct sentences without being taught the rules of grammar overtly. It seems that children have some inbuilt mechanisms helping them to look out for syntax, and to create rules from their experiences. As you saw in the previous chapter, children create 'hypotheses' when building a body of knowledge which they modify as these hypotheses are challenged by experiences. So in building a body of knowledge of syntax, the first hypotheses is probably something like, 'when something happened in the past, the doing word has '–ed' added on.' (I cry, I cried; she helps, she helped). This works for a while until something like 'hurt' or 'build' comes along and hurted or builded is discovered to be wrong, so a modifying hypotheses is added whereby some verbs can have '–t' as their past tense ending. Then there are all the irregular verbs, like run, drink, to be... all 180 of which need to be learnt individually.

Interestingly parents don't tend to correct early syntactical mistakes, which suggests that all this working out of rules is happening in the child's own thought processes. 'Want biscuit' is generally accepted (although most would prompt the child to add 'please'). Parents tend only to correct if the semantics are incorrect, so 'there dog' would only be corrected if in fact the child was pointing to a cat, with the parent saying something like, 'no, that's a cat,' but if the object is actually a dog, we would accept this grammatically incomplete sentence. What parents seem to do to help with syntax is what we call 're-casting' – giving the child alternative ways of talking about the object. So we repeat the sentence back, expanded and re-casted. 'There dog' would be expanded to a response from the parent such as, 'Yes, there is the dog' or re-casted 'Where is the dog?'

Pragmatics

We have thought about how toddlers can break up the stream of sound into understandable chunks, how parents, using Motherese, help the child understand how to chunk the sound waves, but actually none of us gains all the meanings we need simply from the sound waves. Meaning comes from context, from the social situation in which we are communicating, and meaning also comes from other clues such as body language. Although there is no firm agreement about exactly how much meaning we pick up non-verbally, psychologists would probably accept that it is at least 65 per cent.

When two people from the same culture are talking to each other, their bodies are also moving in 'interactional synchrony' – mirroring each other's head and hand movements and general posture. You can tell how emotionally involved people are by watching them talk together, even if you cannot hear what they are saying, simply by observing this body language dance. Babies have been observed moving in synchrony with the human speech going on around them – whichever language it is – while they do not do this dance for non-speech sounds.

For the first 15–18 months of life, babies and mothers also practise non-verbal communication together, creating a unique dialogue, referred to as 'intersubjectivity', developing a very sensitive attunement to each other's emotional state, starting with 'gaze coupling' – taking turns in eye contact, smiling and movement as a kind of non-verbal communicative dance of interaction. It has been suggested that the separation anxiety, which babies show at around eight months, is not about fear of loss of affection or love, but about the fact that the baby has learned to communicate with his mother in a form that is highly specific to the two of them. A fear of a stranger approaching or his mother disappearing is because he has only learnt to communicate with one other person.

So when we think about babies acquiring language, we can think about them mastering a social world onto which they 'map' language, starting with this early exchange of eye contact (mutual gaze) and smiles, which develops into joint attention, where at around six months, babies will follow their mother's gaze to see what she is looking at. Then there is the emergence of shared gestures: by nine months, babies will start pointing at objects to communicate. They will reach for an object while looking at their mother, thus saying non-verbally, 'give that to me!' This 'joint attention' stage is crucial – mothers will now name objects that they are both paying attention to, and thus the baby can start to copy and accumulate a vocabulary of named objects. These interactions are referred to as the Language Acquisition Support System, and there is evidence that when these early experiences of turn-taking and shared interaction do not happen, language development is delayed.

At the same time as all this social communication of turn taking, exchanging smiles and playing games is happening, parents are also working with their babies' vocalizations, interpreting them and imposing meaning on them. Babies first start to vocalize at around three months with general cooing – vowel sounds like oooh, ahhh, creating a sort of internal map of 'sound to mouth shape', copying the vowels they have heard and practising them. Parents respond, cooing back and talking, introducing their babies to that turn-taking vocal dialogue.

At around seven to eight months (when your baby has developed the prototypical vowel) he starts to string consonant and vowel together into a stream of babble. So we hear babababababa or mamamama or dadadada. Whether babies mean anything or not by these sounds is a matter of debate among psychologists but parents do attribute meaning to these sounds; 'Listen, he is saying Mummy!' – and in most cultures the childhood name for the person who is usually the primary care-giver sounds very like that first babble (Mummy, Maman, Mutti etc,).

When babies reach about a year old, parents start giving a running commentary on their actions. 'Are you giving me that cup? Yes, you are giving me that cup. What a helpful boy' and so on. Again a cause perhaps for embarrassment if done in front of other adults, but something parents do spontaneously and naturally when faced with a child of that age. And yet what adults are doing here is teaching their children culturally specific meanings. They are also focusing on what is important to understand about that language; so Korean-speaking mothers, in order to help their children get to grips with the fact that all the different verb endings convey different meanings, will emphasize verbs often omitting nouns, while English-speaking mothers will focus on nouns more.

How does your child know which word applies to what? If, for instance, as above you say, 'Are you giving me that cup?' how does he know you mean cup and not drink or liquid or red thing? We think that children assume three basic things about words:

- They refer to whole objects (cup rather than handle of cup).
- They refer to classes of objects rather than particular instances of objects (cup rather than a particular cup).
- That objects only have one name.

If they assume this then any new word applies to one category, and then additional new words are meant to refine that category.

How children learn to speak, step by step

- Up to 12 months – learning prototypical sounds, practising prototypical vowels in babbling at around three months, practising prototypical vowel and consonant combinations (dadada) at around eight months. Meanwhile parents are reinforcing this by interpreting the sounds into words and appearing pleased with the baby's effort. Parents are also teaching their babies to communicate non-verbally though body language.
- Around 12 months – first words produced (it is easy to miss these). From now on babbling will sound culturally specific; English-speaking babies will sound English when they babble.
- Up to 18 months – toddlers use single words with great flexibility, applying the same word to many objects with an internal logic. 'Dada' for all men for instance, 'dog' might be used to describe all animals or perhaps all moving objects or brown things – whatever makes sense and is useful to the baby.
- Beyond 18 months – there is a rapid accumulation of vocabulary; with children pointing at everything and asking for its name, referred to as 'fast mapping'. Children typically have only about 20 words at 18 months but this has increased to an average of 200 by about 21 months. It seems, too, that words acquired at this age are remembered for a long time.

- As vocabulary increases, children start combining words into phrases, usually two-word 'telegraphic' speech – so called as it sounds like a telegram, for instance, 'dog gone', 'shoe off'. Note that this telegraphic speech is usually in the grammatically correct order, so they don't say 'gone dog'. Single words can also be used to express ideas, referred to as 'holophrases' – typically 'more' actually means 'can I have some more of that please', for instance.
- By two years – children are regularly stringing three or four words together, using grammatical rules.
- Somewhere between three and five years – children will probably have a vocabulary of over 1,000 words, and will be able to carry on conversations, though the topic of conversation will still be rooted in the here and now.

Helping your toddler

As your baby grows, he will, with encouragement, become a chatterbox, and love to strike up conversations with everybody he meets. For this to progress beyond 'toddler conversation', so that he can grow up to feel confident and to have the natural inclination to talk to others, you need to give him plenty of practice. Listen to him, talk back, and value what he says. At the same time, try to improve his listening skills through games. Teach him not to interrupt and to take turns. Begin to demonstrate good manners – say 'please', 'thank you' and 'pardon' to him as you would to others.

When your child starts to attempt to speak, it is important that you don't correct his pronunciation. It will improve with practice of its own accord, but research shows that parents who keep criticizing their children's attempts to speak by correcting them, will discourage their children so they will grow up with smaller vocabularies than other children. It is better to 're-cast' it – repeat it back and expand it.

Case history: Yvonne and Emma

Yvonne's friend has been taking her baby to baby-signing classes and swears by it, even though her baby is not deaf. She is encouraging Yvonne to come along and bring baby Emma. Is this the latest fad, or will it actually help Emma to speak?

Answer: teaching your baby sign language is the latest rage. Is it worth it? Proponents of baby signing methods claim that babies whose parents sign with them (as well as talk to them) communicate earlier through signs AND spoken word. They claim that developing two-way communication from early on reduces miscommunication and thereby reducing the child's frustration and tantrums. They also claim improved IQ sustained to age eight. We don't know whether these children are more advanced simply because their parents are making more effort to help their babies, or whether it is the signing per se that helps, but having said that, the baby signing classes might be fun for Yvonne and Emma, and anything which promotes activities between mother and baby as well as socializing with other babies is usually a good thing, and there is certainly no harm in her going along if she finds the idea appealing.

(See *Teach Yourself Baby Signing*, Jane Jarvis)

Summary of this chapter

- Children are born with inbuilt learning mechanisms: to pay attention to speech; to listen out for rhythms, patterns and repetitions; and with some sort of innate understanding of grammar. However, adults too have inbuilt mechanisms driving us to teach children in ways that will work exactly as needed.
- Parents build on what the baby is already doing, fine tuning if you like, games, interactions, communication. As the baby grasps what is going on, it becomes more of a mutual interaction, often initiated by the baby.

20

how memory works

In this chapter you will learn:

- about the different types of memory
- how knowledge is stored in the brain
- why children can't remember much about their early childhood
- what you can do to help your child retain and recall stored knowledge.

If knowledge is to be useful to your toddler, it needs to be stored in her brain and accessed when needed. This is the task of memory, without which we cannot recall previous experiences, cannot use our knowledge, cannot in fact use language appropriately. So how does memory work, and is it different for children?

How memories are stored in the brain

All memories are stored as patterns of synaptic change somewhere in the brain. In fact if you like, our entire nervous system including the spinal cord and all the peripheral nerves participate in forming memories, because information storage is a fundamental property of neurons, and all nerve cells are capable of modifying themselves according to patterns of electrical activity. Experience is continually rewiring our brains. Active synapses and pathways are strengthened and inactive ones weakened according to the sights, sounds, feelings and events of daily life, and thus memories are laid down and strengthened by changing the density of connections.

It is tempting to imagine that memories are stored like music was stored on vinyl – in grooves – only in this case the grooves are neurons. However, biological memories, unlike those stored mechanically on vinyl record or through a digital recording device like a computer, are highly dynamic and continuously changing with subsequent experiences and influences. We don't have little clumps of neurons each corresponding to a unique memory distributed evenly over our brains; the stronger the connections or synapses between one group of neurons and another, the more easily that memory can be triggered and therefore the more readily it is available.

The different types of memory

Fundamentally there are three different types of memory: the sensory register, the short-term or working memory, and long-term memory.

If we imagine that everything going on around us is potential stimuli or input, anything we notice or pay attention to registers fleetingly in the 'sensory register'. This is a very brief storage facility, which can hold onto thousands of pieces of information, but only for two seconds or less and it is continually being over-written by more input.

From this we select some of the information; whatever is significant at that moment in time, for processing in our working memory, which lasts longer but has a limited capacity. You will have noticed the limitations of your short-term memory when trying to hang on to a phone number – you have to keep repeating it to keep it in your working memory, and if it is too long you just won't be able to retain it. In fact, psychologists have discovered that you can hold onto seven chunks of information in your short-term memory, plus or minus two.

Important information or data in our working memory is then processed mostly via the hippocampus, a part of the primitive brain, to be stored in the long-term memory, which has unlimited capacity and indefinite storage time. In fact, it is a matter of speculation as to whether we ever forget anything that is in our long-term memory, and perhaps 'forgetting' is simply about not being able to retrieve what is stored. Long-term memory survives all sorts of things; sleep, being in a coma, etc. It is stored in different areas of the brain in different ways, as we shall see, and there are several types of long-term memory, but the two most important are as follows:

Procedural or implicit memory: this is the unconscious memory of things we can do, skills we have mastered, like walking, swimming, riding a bike or even driving a car and playing the piano. These are stored in the larger and more primitive parts of our brain and are thus more robust; these are usually unimpaired in cases of amnesia or extensive brain damage. Implicit memories are recalled or remembered literally and exactly, and are laid down by repetition and rehearsal. Most of what your toddler can do at the moment is because of information stored in her procedural memory, which has been laid down through play, imitation, trial and error.

Episodic or explicit memory: this is our conscious memory of events, which develops relatively late in childhood. These memories are highly individual and are arguably what makes us unique from every other person on the planet. What is particularly interesting about these memories are that they are not recalled literally. They tend to be re-categorized and modified every time they are recalled.

Storing and retrieving learnt skills

Procedural or implicit memories (which you probably think of as skills) are eventually stored in the brain's autopilot, the cerebellum, but while we are learning them the hippocampus is crucial, acting like an internalized practice device, liaising between our working memory and the cerebellum. We need to repeat actions over and over before our brain can master the co-ordination between sense and movement, and the hippocampus acts like the stabilizers on a bike while we are mastering these skills, working as some kind of internalized practice device.

For example, when we are learning to drive a car, we will probably need to use a large amount of working memory, but as we practise, we need to use less working memory, until driving becomes fairly automatic, and is controlled by the cerebellum at an unconscious level. However, in certain circumstances, say driving on a busy motorway, or driving abroad, more attention is needed to the task in hand, so we start using our working memory again, leaving us less 'space' for other things like chatting, or even changing CDs!

Why can't we remember anything from our infancy?

While events in our infancy may shape the person we become, we have no conscious memory of these events, because the ability to store episodic (explicit) long-term memories, which are generally spread all over the cerebral cortex, develops relatively late in childhood. So early experiences never make it into long-term memory banks because the brain's recording machinery isn't functioning yet. Even if you are one of the rare people who claim to remember events before your second birthday, you are in fact recalling memories which were stored much later than this, probably from photographs, imagination, or from being told about events at a later date. They will feel real, but as we shall see, children are not capable of recalling these early memories, and often find it difficult to distinguish between reality and fantasy.

How memory develops

- In the beginning babies have primitive memory skills, storing information at an automatic unconscious level, which lasts for relatively short periods of time. They can **recognize** things they have seen before when presented with them again (like their parents' faces, for instance) but can't recall them when they are not present.

- Conscious memories emerge at around six months old, when the baby can **recall** things that are not actually there (so these are conscious memories by definition). At this stage, babies become anxious about being separated, they become aware that objects continue to exist when not being seen – this means they have some internal image of that person or object stored in their brain which they can retrieve. This is still fairly fleeting, short-term and probably not within their conscious control.

- At around eight or nine months they show the first signs of more flexible, deliberate storage of information, when the activity in their frontal lobes increases.

- These episodes grow longer and increasingly conscious throughout the pre-school years until in their early school years they become aware of their own memory skills and begin to use them in a truly mature way – to intentionally study and acquire new information. So memory development is what makes formal school learning possible.

How psychologists have discovered what babies can remember

We cannot ask babies what they are remembering, but one experiment set out to find out how long babies could retain information. The experimenter did something unusual in front of a baby, like touching a particular object to his forehead, and the baby was then shown the object again after some delay to see if she could remember and imitate that behaviour.

- Nine-month-old babies imitated the experimenter up to 24 hours later.

- Thirteen-month-old babies could remember and copy a week later.

- Fifteen-month-old babies could still imitate the action after a four month delay.

Although imitation is not necessarily a conscious act, so the babies might not be recalling the event in the way we do, the experiment does demonstrate that babies can remember things for a long time and copy our actions quite some time later.

Can babies remember trauma?

It is a source of angst among some parents as to whether their babies will be traumatized in some ways by early experiences. Although we all know that we cannot consciously recall events from our early childhood, the question is, are they there, lurking in our brains, driving us to behave in certain ways? Certainly psychoanalysts like Freud and his followers believe they do.

The truth is that it's hard to answer this completely, but we do know that traumatic infancies can produce emotionally traumatized adults. For instance, the experiences of neglect, inconsistency or abuse will affect the way they behave in adult relationships. We don't fully understand how emotional memories are laid down but they are stored in the more primitive parts of the brain and are very robust.

Thankfully, most babies are not subject to emotionally disturbed infancies, and unless it was highly traumatic, one-off experiences leave little trace. Although these register in the amygdala, the part of the primitive brain which is responsible for instant reactions to situations of danger, it is only if the baby suffers from a chronic lack of positive social interaction with others that her capacity to override her primitive responses may not develop. The links between the prefrontal cortex and amygdala may be pruned because they are not well established, and then these links are too weak to inhibit the amygdala's fearful responses leaving her prone to anxieties and fears.

High levels of cortisol (stress hormone) can damage the hippocampus, which is why people under stress can become absent-minded or scatty; their capacity to retrieve information being reduced. Too much cortisol at an early age can shrink the hippocampus, and people with smaller hippocampi are more vulnerable to post-traumatic stress disorder.

Babies who are touched and held a great deal in infancy can cope more easily with stress as adults. Firstly children with secure attachments do not release high levels of cortisol under stress, whereas insecure children do, and secondly those who are touched and held a great deal in babyhood have been found to have an abundance of cortisol receptors in the hippocampus so that when cortisol levels rise under future stress, there are more receptors to receive it and they can cope more easily with stress.

Using memory in everyday life – scripts

To operate in the world, we need to know when we are encountering a new version of a familiar experience. Without this knowledge stored in and retrieved from memory, each experience would have to be treated as if it were completely new. So, for instance, each time we are faced with a meal it is actually a different experience; there may be different food arranged in a different way, on a different plate; we might be eating in a restaurant or a friend's house rather than in our own kitchen, but we do not have to learn how to cope each time.

What we do is organize our experiences so that we have a 'script' of actions to follow, and this frees up our working memories. So you might have a script of your journey to work, which involves a large series of linked events; putting coat on, locking front door, walking to the station, etc. – all of which can be done on what feels like 'automatic pilot' but is in fact a script in your memory. Your toddler will need to develop these scripts too.

Experimenters asked children to describe what happened in different eating contexts: lunch at nursery, dinner at home and going to McDonalds. Most of the children mentioned the same things for each event, focusing on main actions such as eating, leaving an 'open slot' for more specific information if required such as what was eaten on Thursday say. But they all reported paying for the food at the **end** of the meal at McDonalds, suggesting that they had a general script about eating out (in most restaurants, payment is made at the end) rather than a specific memory of eating at McDonalds (where you pay when you order your food). It is interesting to note that this paper was written in 1981, when McDonalds was less ubiquitous – presumably if the experiment were to be repeated today, the script might well assume paying for food first whatever the restaurant!

Using memory in everyday life – narrative

When we are thinking or remembering, we often have an internal dialogue going on in our heads; much of our memory seems to involve verbal skills, and as toddlers can't say very much, it has been suggested that this also explains why they can't remember very much.

However, toddlers can talk about episodes of their favourite programmes that they hadn't seen since *before* they could talk, so language is not a prerequisite for storing conscious memories. We now think that toddlers can remember much more than they can talk about, but are just unable to verbalize these memories at first, and eventually, as verbal skills develop, these memories are lost to recall.

Once we have developed the art of narrative, we are then capable of seeing relationships between events and can place our own personal recollections into a framework of time, place and causality. It is at this point only that our memories can survive the transition from childhood to later life. So infantile amnesia is not to do with passage of time, but is because either the memories were never stored in the first place or else they are stored but inaccessible.

Using memory in everyday life – conscious strategies

Retrieval is something we all struggle with from time to time, and what many of us do is to develop strategies. For instance, if you were trying to remember someone's name you might try running through all the letters of the alphabet and seeing if it triggers something. Trying to get the synapses near that name to fire is probably what is happening, and it is possible that the name is going to be stored with some attention paid to the initial.

If you have ever experienced the problem of arriving in a room ready to do something and completely forgetting what it is you were about to do, you might have discovered that a good way to trigger recall is to retrace your steps until you reach the place where you made the initial decision to do something. So you arrive back in the bathroom, see the broken light bulb, and remember you were going to look for a new one.

When you are trying to remember a phone number and you don't have a piece of paper to hand, you might chant the number out loud over and over until you find pen and paper (rehearsal). This is a strategy that you will have learnt through experience and which can be effective in remembering a long string of abstract symbols, i.e. numbers.

We also group information together to help recall (e.g. trying to remember a shopping list by grouping similar items – 'I need bread and milk from the supermarket, stamps and envelopes from the post office and then into the vets for the worming tablets'). This is called chunking. If you are trying to remember a telephone number you chunk the area code, and then chunk the digits together in twos for the remainder. Some people find acronyms helpful (these are also examples of chunking): you remember the initial letters of a series as one word, for example NATO or Aids. 'FACE' is an acronym which helps children remember the names of the notes which occur in the spaces of sheet music.

> Interestingly it has been suggested that many words are examples of chunking. A new word is often invented by people to replace what was previously a phrase. 'A dictionary is a compendium of chunking over the centuries.' – William H Calvin (1998) *How brains think – the evolution of intelligence* (Phoenix).

Helping your child to develop strategies

We are usually aware of the limitations of our own memories and the need for strategies, but it takes children some time to realize they have limited capacity; it is not until around age eight that they can predict their own limitations. In order to remember, children need to learn to pay attention to the right thing, which they become more skilled at with age. They also need to develop encoding strategies.

Ask your two-year-old toddler to go upstairs, go into the bathroom and fetch a toothbrush and toothpaste, and they may have forgotten it all before they even reach the foot of the stairs. They have not yet developed an effective encoding strategy like rehearsal.

In one study, three-year-olds were better at retrieving a hidden toy dog if the experimenter explicitly asked them at the time of hiding it to remember where the dog is. So you can help your toddler improve her memory by teaching her strategies.

Children whose mothers put greater demand on their memories, who frequently question them about past events or probe their growing body of general knowledge, perform better on tests of recall. What is happening is that this questioning helps the child to focus on thinking about the 'who, what, when, where, how and why' issues; to think about events in terms of time and causality which is ultimately how we recall facts and events later on.

- Help your toddler to develop her memory by talking over events and sharing experiences. Perhaps you could make a point of talking about the day as part of her bedtime routine.
- Teach her to pay attention by playing games like sorting shapes and doing puzzles, and getting her to sort objects in different ways, e.g. according to colour, shape, size, etc.
- Playing hide and seek with teddy bears will help her to pay attention to the look of things.
- As you go about your daily life together, try to do an occasional running commentary on what you are both doing. This helps your child to develop her own internal narrative, which is what she will eventually need to organize her memory.

Case history: Marion and Rose

Rose has got to go into hospital for an operation, and Marion is worried about Rose being traumatized by the memory of the pain as well as being separated from her. She has terrible memories of her time in hospital as a child; of being scared, lonely and in pain, and does not want to put Rose through the same.

Answer: hospitals have changed beyond recognition now. Children's wards are bright cheerful places with lots of things to do. Parents are encouraged to stay with their children as much as possible, including overnight. Pain relief management is also far superior, and the chances are that Rose will feel minimal discomfort.

In addition, given that Rose is so much younger than Marion was when she was admitted, the chances are she will not remember much about it afterwards. But as long as Marion can stay with her as much as possible, to entertain and comfort her and to ensure that all her needs are met, the time may well be far happier than she might imagine.

It is worth Marion talking to the nurses on the ward before the visit to ask what sorts of things she could bring to help Rose settle, and find out what arrangements are in hand for her to stay overnight.

False memories

Interestingly, until recently, people have assumed that young children do not make reliable witnesses as they have inaccurate memories, but in fact young children make fewer errors than older children, they just can't remember as much, and they are far more susceptible to leading questions.

They sometimes have difficulty recalling the source of a memory and this means that they may confuse something that actually happened with something they had only thought about. Just getting young children to think about invented events can lead to them believing that they actually happened. This false remembering may happen because they encode less information about an event than an adult, or it may be that because of working memory constraints, they have more gaps that can be filled in by suggestive questioning. Young children also don't like not to answer if an adult asks a question, so they will sometimes answer a question they don't know to please the adult concerned.

Summary of this chapter

- Experiences are stored in the brain as patterns of change in our nervous system; this is how knowledge or memory happens.
- There are several different types of memory including short-term, limited memory, long-term implicit memory (skills) and long-term explicit memory (conscious recall of events).
- We can't remember the events of infancy because our ability to store explicit memories has not yet formed. Emotional traumas and skills are 'remembered' unconsciously because they are stored in a more primitive part of the brain.
- You can help your toddler develop her memory through games, stories and by teaching her explicit strategies.

21

becoming self-aware

In this chapter you will learn:
- how your toddler develops self-awareness
- what he understands about himself and other people
- why your toddler is not very good at telling fibs.

One of the most difficult things for psychologists to discover, strangely enough, is what is really going on inside someone else's head. For years they have grappled with what is called the 'theory of mind'; so called because of course we can never know for sure that other people do actually have minds as we cannot directly experience them, we simply have to infer it from their behaviour. Understanding when this 'theory of mind' develops in children means we can understand when they become self-aware, when they become conscious of others, how they might understand the world from other people's points of view, which would allow them to feel empathy and also, of course, to deceive.

Traditionally psychologists thought the theory of mind developed quite late, but we are now beginning to realize that even toddlers have some understanding about other people who share similar, or different, perspectives from their own.

Investigating what a toddler might believe about himself is fairly difficult, but we know that from birth, babies imitate adults and prefer to look at pictures of other human beings so there must be some awareness of 'like me', however this might be expressed in a baby's head.

A shared perspective

The act of pointing implies something quite interesting about toddlers' understanding of themselves and others. If you point at something, by about a year old your child will look precisely to where you are pointing. Try it with a cat or dog and they will simply look at your finger. Your toddler, however, understands the intention behind the pointing. And when he points at something himself, he looks at your face to check that you are looking where he intends. There is an implicit understanding about a shared view of the world.

This all makes sense because as a baby becomes mobile, he needs to pay attention to how people relate to objects in case he encounters something dangerous. A toddler who encounters a new object will first look at his mother to see her reaction, and this will determine what he does. If she looks afraid, perhaps it is best to avoid that object for the time being.

One experimenter had mothers look in boxes and show either joy or disgust, then hand the boxes to their one-year-old babies. The babies happily reached into the box if the mothers showed joy, but would not open the box if they reacted with disgust.

These babies are interpreting the facial expressions and extrapolating from this some implication for themselves. Babies will also imitate what grown-ups do with objects – for instance they will hold a toy telephone to their ear even though they have no understanding of why their parents do this or what they get out of it.

So we can conclude that quite early on, babies or toddlers know that they might share perspectives with others about the world.

Developing a sense of self

Babies around nine to 12 months will look longer and smile more at pictures of themselves and by 15 to 18 months babies will talk about themselves, for instance, as 'baby,' or use their own name to label pictures of themselves. But do they really understand what this name means, or do they understand that the two-dimensional object is a representation of themselves? Psychologists devised what they call 'the mirror test' to work out if babies really do recognize themselves. Babies aged from nine months sit with their mothers in front of a large mirror and after a minute or so the mothers wipes the baby's face, and in the process, surreptitiously puts some rouge on the end of the baby's nose. The babies are then put in front of the mirror again to see how they respond.

While at all ages the babies smile at the reflection and point or reach out for the mirror, the younger babies do not touch their own noses when they see the rouge. By 15 to 18 months a few of the babies reach for their own noses having seen themselves in the mirror but not many. However, by 21 to 24 months most babies reach for their *own* noses when they see their rouged reflection. So it seems that it is not until after 18 months that babies understand that the mirror is showing them a reflection or representation of themselves.

Babies love looking at themselves in the mirror, in photos or on videos. You can have an entertaining afternoon together looking at photos and videos and talking about what you are both seeing.

Knowing that others are different

Part of developing a sense of yourself as a unique individual must involve understanding that other people are different. We know that babies have some sense of people as 'like me'; they will copy adults from birth, smile at them and as we have seen, will use other people to get a sense of how to respond to new things in the world, but when do they begin to understand that there might be a difference between people? More particularly when do they begin to understand that people's minds might be different from their own?

In one experiment, young toddlers were shown two bowls of food, one full of delicious biscuits, the other full of raw broccoli. They preferred the biscuits, naturally. The experimenter then tasted each bowl and made a delighted face for one, and a disgusted face for the other, and asked the toddlers to give her some more. When she suggested she liked the biscuits, naturally enough the toddlers gave her these. However when she suggested she preferred the broccoli, she found that 14-month-old toddlers would still give her the biscuits, but 18-month-old toddlers would give her the broccoli. So by a year-and-a-half, children are beginning to understand that some people may have different desires from their own.

Why toddlers deliberately do what you don't want them to do!

The broccoli and biscuit experimenters suggest that two-year-olds are deliberately doing things that you don't want them to do as part of a systematic exploration of how their desires and yours may conflict, which is of course a fairly new and interesting concept for them. If your toddler has just discovered that you and he think differently and have different wants and desires, it makes complete sense that he will keep trying different things just to see where you really differ. You may well notice that your toddler often misbehaves (does what you don't want him to do) more often when you are actually there to witness it and to respond. This may also be why showing minimal reaction to naughtiness works – if you don't respond when he misbehaves, he loses interest in doing it.

Understanding differing perspectives

An interesting experiment had 18-month-old toddlers look at a new object while their mothers looked at a *different* object and said, 'oh look, a dax!' (a word made up for this experiment). The experimenter then put both objects in front of the child and asked, 'show me the dax' and the child indicated the object that the mother had been looking at, rather than the thing he had been looking at when she spoke. If children of this age did not grasp that other people might have different points of view, they would have thought the dax was the object they were looking at when their mothers did the naming. But it makes sense that for children to acquire vocabulary, they would need to have this sophisticated understanding of different points of view.

When two-year-olds are asked to show another person a picture, they will angle it so it is visible from that person's perspective. They also understand that if people have their hands over their eyes, they would not be able to see something, or if they hid an object, that person would not be able to see it. Three-year-olds also know that if person A has looked into a box, she will know what was in it, but if person B has not looked, she will not know. So they can appreciate that people can have different knowledge about the world, and sometimes this might not be complete.

Encourage your toddler to see the world from other people's points of view, by talking about how people feel or react to different situations. Being explicit about motives and feelings is important in helping your child to develop emotional intelligence.

The ability to deceive

The reason psychologists until recently did not believe children had a developed theory of mind arose from the classical Sally–Anne experiment. Children watch two dolls, Sally and Anne. Sally puts a marble in a basket, then leaves. Anne then takes the marble out and puts it in a box. Sally then returns. The child is asked, 'Where will Sally look for her marble?' Typically four-year-olds will (correctly) say that Sally will look in the basket, while three-year-olds will (incorrectly) say she will look in the box. This suggested that children younger than four could not understand that someone else might have a different perspective. (Interestingly, children with autistic spectrum disorders – see Chapter 22 – usually fail the Sally–Anne test.)

However, in another experiment similar to the Sally–Anne test, children are shown a closed box of Smarties and asked what it is in it. They nearly always say, 'Smarties'. The lid is then taken off to reveal pencils. The lid is then replaced and the child is asked what her friend will think is in the box. Four-year-olds will typically say Smarties, but younger children will say pencils.

However, when you ask the children what *they* thought was in the box before, the four-year-olds will say Smarties but the three-year-olds will say pencils. They seem not to grasp that previously they had a false belief. So the problem was not lack of insight into other people's minds, but lack of insight into the concept of having false beliefs about the world.

This is linked, of course, with the ability to deceive. Primates are capable of this deception. For instance, say a chimpanzee finds a nice stash of bananas when another chimp arrives on the scene. The first chimp is capable of walking away from the food, pretending there was nothing of interest and waiting till the second chimp leaves, then returning to the bananas to eat them. (Meanwhile, however, the second chimp might equally have only pretended to leave and was in fact hiding behind a tree, so when the first chimp uncovers the bananas, he emerges, chases that chimp away, and scoffs the bananas himself!)

So our closest relatives – the chimps – are capable of implanting false beliefs in each other (and thus are demonstrating awareness of the mind of another) but it seems from the Sally–Anne and Smarties experiments, that three-year-olds cannot grasp this same concept. Another experiment was devised to see if children were capable of implanting a false belief in another's mind, similar to the chimps. Children were told they could choose a sticker, but only after a mean puppet had chosen one (and the children discovered that this mean puppet would normally chose the one the children wanted out of spite). When asked in front of the mean puppet, which sticker they wanted, the five-year-olds pointed to a sticker they did not want, thus deceiving the mean puppet into taking the wrong one, but the three- and four-year-olds would point out the sticker they did want, and thus lose it to the mean puppet. On subsequent tests, the four-year-olds quickly modified their behaviour to deceive the puppet, but the poor three-year-olds could not do it, and lost the stickers repeatedly. They could not work out how to implant a false belief in the puppet.

So young children find it difficult to grasp the concept of false belief, or to create a false belief in someone else. However, it could be that language is the key here. Children with delayed speech or hearing problems will have more problems with false-belief tests, while children who have more opportunities to mix with siblings and other children tend to do better on false-belief tasks, probably because they are more likely to talk about thoughts and beliefs with other children.

The other reason it may take so long to accept the concept of false belief is that it requires children to understand the nature of mental representations – that these are copies of reality, not reality. Young children have different concepts of reality; a three-year-old will accept anything they see as real – optical illusions, pictures of fictional characters and so on. But by four and especially five years of age they begin to understand imagination, optical illusions and to understand that outward appearances can be doubted. It seems that as their brains develop and there is increased communication between the hemispheres, the linking of the perceptual skills in the right brain with analytical skills in the left brain allow children to doubt the evidence of their senses, and to realize that their eyes can deceive them.

Being good at fibs

In order to deceive others, children need to be aware of their own mental states, and this allows them to project onto others using an 'as if' pretence mechanism. Before they can do this, they need to develop:

1 Self-awareness, which emerges at around 18 to 20 months (see beginning of this chapter).
2 The capacity for pretence, which emerges during their second year (see Chapter 21).
3 The ability to distinguish reality from pretence.

Summary of this chapter

- Your toddler will gradually build up a 'theory of mind' starting with shared understandings and then developing into an understanding that other people may have different points of view.
- Psychologists are still trying to clarify exactly what is going on, but it does seem clear that children understand that other people have different and separate minds with different perspectives, far earlier than was previously believed.

22

when you worry about your toddler's development

In this chapter you will learn:
- about some of the developmental disorders like dyslexia, ADHD and autistic spectrum disorders
- how you might spot the early signs of these problems in your child
- what you should do if you think your toddler needs extra help.

All children progress at different rates, and some children will be more physical and less communicative for instance; some children are very sociable, others prefer being on their own. While it is completely natural to worry about your child, and to want to help him develop to the best of his abilities, there may be signs that he will need some extra help even at this stage.

The common problems

There are a growing number of children who have a diagnosis of some sort of learning disorder; the more common are: ADHD (Attention Deficit Hyperactivity Disorder); spectrum disorders ranging from Asperger's Syndrome through to classic autism; and dyslexia or dyspraxia. While these may all sound like completely different problems, in fact there are links and overlaps with all of them, and many children can be diagnosed as having more than one syndrome. One thing they have in common, too, is that they are all descriptions of a group of behaviours or problems, rather than illnesses per se, and they range in degree of severity. Many children show some signs of these syndromes sometimes; children who are formally diagnosed simply have more of the signs, more often. Diagnosis is usually sought when the child's behaviour is having a negative effect on their life.

It could be argued that every human being has each of these disorders to some extent, and children who are labelled simply have more extreme versions. As they are not illnesses, they cannot be treated and cured, but instead need practical help, and some children, given help early enough may well overcome any problems completely.

Having said that, it would be rare for a toddler to be formally diagnosed for any of these conditions, and the purpose of this chapter is just to give you some indication of what might be in store for you if you suspect your toddler has more problems than his peers.

ADHD (ADD) – Attention Deficit (Hyperactivity) Disorder

There are many misconceptions about ADHD or ADD. A child who is 'bouncing off the walls' may not have it, while a dreamy child, who isn't progressing at school, may in fact have ADD (Attention Deficit Disorder without hyperactivity).

The typical ADD or ADHD child is impulsive, easily bored or distracted, disorganized, has difficulty following a set of directions, and yet can concentrate intensely on something that grabs their interest. They usually have poor social skills and so have problems making or keeping friends. As you can see, most toddlers could be described as ADHD to some extent; and a classic ADHD child behaves to a great extent like a manic toddler.

It is unlikely, therefore, that a toddler would be diagnosed as having ADHD or ADD, and even older children need a detailed assessment from an educational psychologist. However, ADHD children need behaviour management strategies first and foremost, and these are just as effective with difficult to manage, non-ADHD children or toddlers.

Tackling ADHD with behaviour strategies

All children respond well to boundaries, and an ADHD child needs structure more than most. However, the ADHD child will take boundaries as a personal challenge, and will constantly push at them, past the point where most other children would back off. Parents need to be really strong and be prepared to stand their ground on boundaries and rules far more than they would have to with their other children.

As a parent of an ADHD child, you will need to invest time in discussing and agreeing rules and structures with your partner and children, but your child will thrive. It is better to start by targeting the biggest problem areas – don't attempt to sort everything out at once. Bedtimes or leaving the house – whichever time of day is worst is the one to start with. See if you can figure out what triggers your child's behaviour – often transitions are problematic; for instance, going from home to school.

The ADHD child loves attention, but most of the attention they get is negative; shouts, screams, 'don't do that!' You need to starve him of attention when he misbehaves, and go mad with positive attention when he gets something right.

He also enjoys the stimulation of an argument; as arguing involves far more attention than complying. The 'broken record' response is really useful – in a flat monotone, keep repeating yourself, 'No, you are not allowed the TV until you have got dressed.' Remember the ADHD loathes boredom, and if you are responding in a boring voice, he will quickly lose interest.

The '1,2,3 Magic' technique works really well with all children, especially those with ADHD. It involves counting out, in a firm but unemotional tone, when you want your child to stop doing something. Having told them to stop, if they haven't, you say, 'That's one'. If the behaviour continues, you proceed to, 'That's two'. If they get to three then there are negative consequences – usually time out in their room. The most important part of this technique is that there is no extra communication; no argument, just the counting.

Star charts also work well with ADHD children as they are very goal-orientated. A working star chart will have up to five clear, specific, 'more of…' behaviours as well as up to five 'less of…' behaviours, with the balance weighted so they can win more than lose, so the system is not demoralizing. Start by tackling the biggest problem areas. For example, two pluses for a more of (getting ready for nursery on time) and one minus for a less of (throwing a tantrum). Rewards should be meaningful and attainable; for example, ten pluses = a trip to the swimming pool.

One recent piece of research in London found that young adults are more likely to have grown out of ADHD if their families were accepting and they did not experience too much hostility from other people. The researchers also found that in families with ADHD children, reducing hostility lead to less hyperactivity.

Dyslexia

Dyslexia affects four per cent of the population, and is four times as common in boys. Many children endure several years of failure at school before being diagnosed, while those who slip through the net may never live up to their academic potential, suffering chronic self-esteem problems. Dyslexia has probably always existed, but only in the last few decades have psychologists noticed the existence of a large group of children, who were not 'slow' or 'stupid', but who had great difficulties in reading and spelling. One of the most striking things about these children was that they all had the same type of difficulties, and the term 'dyslexia' – from the Greek for 'bad speech', was coined to describe them.

Although initially all children make reading and spelling mistakes, the mistakes dyslexics make tend to be more bizarre and persistent. Dyslexia has nothing to do with socio-economic or linguistic background, bad teaching or lack of intelligence.

Often dyslexic children are bright and can be very creative; the mistakes they make in reading, writing and spelling occur *despite* these strengths, and are due to underlying difficulties with memory, phonological awareness and information processing. There can also be problems with co-ordination, sequencing, time-keeping, sense of direction and interpersonal skills.

How might you spot the early signs of dyslexia?

Most dyslexia is not spotted until school age, but there are signs you can look out for in the pre-school child, and it is worth doing so if you have a family history of dyslexia. Early signs might be:

- Persistent jumbled phrases, e.g. cobblers' club for toddlers' club.
- An inability to remember the label for known objects, e.g. table, chair.
- Difficulty learning nursery rhymes and rhyming words, e.g. cat, mat and sat.
- Later than expected speech development.
- A child who may have walked early but did not crawl – was a bottom shuffler or a tummy wriggler.
- Persistent difficulties in getting dressed efficiently and putting shoes on the correct feet.
- A child who enjoys being read to, but shows no interest in letters or words.
- A child who is often accused of not listening or not paying attention.
- Excessive tripping, bumping into things, and falling over.
- Difficulty with catching, kicking or throwing a ball, with hopping and/or skipping.
- Difficulty clapping a simple rhythm.

What to do if you suspect your toddler has dyslexia

You can arrange a private dyslexic assessment; a 20-minute test can assess whether there is a problem, though the formal test, available for school-age children, takes several hours. For more information see page 216. But interestingly enough, it is also worth getting your toddler's vision checked by an optometrist who specializes in children, as a number of dyslexic children could simply have unresolved eye problems, even though they would pass standard vision screening tests.

To be able to read, a child needs not only to see and focus well, but his eyes also need to work together so they're both directed to the same point. Severe problems normally produce a squint, but for dyslexics the problem can be a small and intermittent breakdown; hardest to pick up on screening tests, but where the child would be aware of print moving about on the page, or might not be able to scan well, or to ignore the white spaces between words. He also loses his place and finds it hard to concentrate. Some of these problems will correct themselves as the child grows older, but there are eye exercises which can help.

Irlen Syndrome is another visual problem affecting children with learning difficulties such as dyslexia. The child is sensitive to light, especially that given off by white paper, making black print seem distorted. An easy test involves putting clear coloured plastic sheets over written words; at which point many students say that the print stops 'jumping about'. The optician can then use either a Chromagen or an Intuitive Colorimeter, with 7,000 different tints, to work out exactly which colour helps your child, so they can wear tinted glasses when reading.

Autistic spectrum disorders

While a child with classic and severe autism is profoundly disabled and easy to spot, some children have higher functioning autism – usually called Asperger's sydrome, and while this cannot be cured, as with other developmental disorders, there are ways of helping a child with Asperger's syndrome to function in the everyday world.

Asperger's syndrome children are probably what we might think of as 'eccentric'. They usually have obsessions (special interests) about particular topics, they like routine and order and hate change; they lack social skills and are unable to see the world from other people's point of view. Again this could describe a typical toddler, but other early signs are as follows:

- Slow to speak, and when he does speak will use odd phrases (echololia). Not particularly interested in conversation.
- Poor co-ordination, clumsy.
- Dislikes certain sensations that most people would be able to screen out, e.g. loud noises, bright lights, certain fabrics against the skin.
- Throws a tantrum when a minor change to an expected routine happens.

What to do if you suspect your toddler has Asperger's syndrome

The first step is to talk to your health visitor. Many children are picked up after being referred for speech and language therapy being slow to speak. But for a proper diagnosis, you will need to be seen by a specialist, and referral can be made by your health visitor or through Speech and Language.

Dyspraxia

This used to be called 'clumsy child syndrome'; luckily that pejorative term has fallen out of favour, but the word clumsy is generally what will probably spring to mind. Dyspraxia affects approximately six per cent of the population and up to two per cent severely. Basically the child's co-ordination, gross and fine motor skills are far behind what would be expected at his age, even though other developmental signs are normal.

Symptoms of dyspraxia

- Does not establish left- or right-handedness when expected.
- Does not cope well with PE at school.
- Has difficulty with ball skills and other hand/eye and foot/eye co-ordination activities.
- Listening skills may be poor and the child may not cope with more than one instruction at a time.
- Immature social skills.
- Problems adapting to a structured school routine.
- Slow at dressing (often messy) – unable to tie shoe laces.
- Handwriting is barely legible – immature drawings and poor copying skills.
- Literal use of language.
- Class work is completed slowly and rarely finished.
- Very fidgety, always on the go.
- Easily distressed and very emotional.
- Messy eater and has problems using a knife and fork.
- Often a loner and has problems forming close relationships with peers.

What to do if you suspect your toddler has dyspraxia

As you can see from the list above, you are unlikely to notice dyspraxia in your toddler, and even if you do suspect there is a problem, diagnosis may not happen till later. Dyspraxia is often confused with other conditions like Asperger's syndrome or ADHD, and there is indeed an overlap in symptoms.

What you can do – diet

Because junk food is so ubiquitous in our society, it is hard to establish whether there is cause and effect. Many parents feel that additives in their children's food affect their behaviour, and this makes intuitive sense. However, studies have not always been conclusive. It may be that children who are susceptible to these developmental conditions are also less tolerant of certain foodstuffs. ADHD children do seem to improve if their diet is improved, and Asperger's syndrome children often also have gut and digestive problems, and improving these helps lessen the symptoms of the syndrome.

It is certainly worth being very careful with your toddler's diet, avoiding highly processed foods, keeping blood sugar stable, and keeping an eye on your toddler's bowel habits. You may want to keep a food diary and see if any particular substances have an effect on your child (many parents find the food colouring Tartrazine (E102) makes their child hyperactive, for instance).

There have also been some promising results using long chain polyunsaturated vitamin supplements, like Efalex, which contain fish oil and primrose oil. These seem to help children with ADHD, dyslexia and dyspraxia, while iron and zinc supplements have also helped dyslexics. Consult your doctor before giving your toddler any supplements though.

What you can do – hearing

Many young children can have hearing problems, often caused by glue ear, which if not treated can lead to problems with talking, reading and writing, so it's worth having a thorough hearing test early on. Most of the children with developmental conditions have *listening* problems; in other words, they have problems with auditory attention and processing. Some find it hard to listen to speech with background noise even when their hearing is OK. So cut down on background noise, and be aware that your toddler will need help in developing strategies to pay attention and remember instructions. Have another look at Chapter 20 on memory.

If your toddler is slow to speak, then concentrate on using language as much as possible during the day. Have time where you read books together, go to the library and let your child choose a big pile of new books. Don't worry if the vocabulary looks too advanced; you can tell your own accompanying story.

Remember that children whose parents talk to them more have larger, faster growing vocabularies. But if they hear more 'no', 'don't', 'stop it' and similar prohibitions they have poorer language skills.

- Lots of talking is important, but it must be of the right quality. It must be addressed to the child rather than having your child listening to you talking to others, or listening to nursery workers talking to each other, or having the TV on in the background.
- Your language needs to be simple, clear and positive.
- Children can understand much more than you can say – speak to your toddler in a way that is within reach of his understanding but stretches him a bit.
- Use lots of repetition.
- Don't correct him too much as it gives a negative message; focus on what he is trying to say rather than how he is saying it.

What you can do – balance and co-ordination

Some theorists reckon that developmental disorders happen because certain developmental reflexes have not fully matured. This could explain why all these disorders are often accompanied by poor co-ordination and motor skills problems.

- Cranial osteopathy has been found to help some children with developmental disorders.
- Some parents have found BrainGym exercises helpful. These involve therapy for muscles and posture based on kinesiology principles. See **www.learning-solutions.co.uk/brain_gym_courses.php**.
- You might want to see a neuro-developmental therapist who will assess overall central nervous system functioning including muscle co-ordination, motor skills, visual and auditory abilities, and then offer exercises to correct any problems. See **www.therapyinpraxis.co.uk/html/neuro-developmental.html**.

Games

There is also plenty you could do yourself without spending a penny:

- A game of football or a day at an adventure park involves practising gross motor skills and co-ordination.
- Spinning on a roundabout or playing ring-a-ring-a-roses, helps develop a sense of horizontal movement around a vertical plane.
- Swings, see-saws or rocking horses, slides, somersaults and handstands develop a sense of vertical movement around a horizontal plane.
- Wobbly boards, bouncy castles and trampolines help balance in general.
- Sing nursery rhymes or the alphabet together. Later on, use poems with strong rhyme and rhythm such Dr Seuss and Colin McNaugton.
- The Letterland reading scheme is very good for dyslexics as it contains a strong visual representation of the alphabet. Look out for their floor jigsaw puzzles and audiotapes (**www.letterland.com**).

What causes these developmental disorders?

No one is really sure what causes any of these conditions. There is some evidence that they run in families; you may well have other family members who fit these descriptions. There has also been a suggestion that some may be due to oxygen deprivation at birth. Some researchers point to the inner ear and the cerebellum, which would explain the issues of fine finger control, balance and co-ordination.

Setting boundaries

Phelan, Thomas W. *1-2-3 Magic; Effective Discipline for Children 2–12*.

Healthy eating

Richardson, Dr Alex (2006) *They are what you feed them*, Thorsons. How food can improve your child's behaviour, mood and learning. – Includes helpful recipes.

van Straten, Michael (2001) *Good Mood Food*, Cassell – Although written for adults, the recipes seem tempting enough for kids too, and focus on changing mood, so there are recipes for waking you up, helping you sleep, giving you energy etc.

Whiting, Mary (2003) *Dump the Junk!* Moonscape. Aimed at parents, it is packed with alternatives to junk food, as well as containing lots of tips and strategies to get your child to want to eat healthily.

www.eatwell.gov.uk/agesandstages/children/lunchboxsect – Great ideas for lunch boxes.

Toilet training

Welford, Heather (2003) *Successful Potty Training: A Practical Guide for Today's Parents*, HarperCollins.

Sleep

Deacon, Caroline (2004) *Babycalming – simple solutions for a happy baby*, Thorsons.

Developmental concerns

Attwood, Tony (2000) *Aspergers Syndrome*, Jessica Kingsley Publishers.

British Dyslexia Association: **http://www.bdadyslexia.org.uk**

Dyslexia Action: **http://www.dyslexiaaction.org.uk/**

Hartmann, Thom (2000) *Complete Guide to ADHD*, Underwood Books.

Research on links between food and behaviour: **www.fabresearch.org/**

Richardson, Dr Alex (2006) *They are what you feed them*, Thorsons. How food can improve your child's behaviour, mood and learning. – Includes helpful recipes.

Stordy, Dr Jacqueline (2002) *The remarkable nutritional treatment for ADHD, Dyslexia, and Dyspraxia*, Macmillan. – About the effect of long-chain polyunsaturated fatty acid supplements.

Wallace, Ian (2000) *You & Your ADD Child*, HarperCollins.

Childminding

Childminding in England and Wales: **www.ncma.org.uk**

Scottish childminding association: **http://www.childminding.org**

Nurseries

Daycare Trust: Tel: 020 7840 3350.

Parents' relationships

National Childbirth Trust – Offers antenatal, breastfeeding and postnatal classes, local postnatal support groups, nearly new sales and many other services. NCT Helpline: 0870 444 8707; www.nctpregnancyandbabycare.com

The Parent Connection – Aims to encourage you to think about the importance of your relationship with your child's other parent, whether or not you are still together, and the impact this has on your child: www.theparentconnection.org.uk

Several related websites are also helpful:

One plus one – This website has information and tips to help you to deal with things that may affect your relationship and also other sources of information and support: www.oneplusone.org.uk

Parentline Plus – A national charity that works with parents to offer help and support through an innovative range of free, flexible, responsive services – shaped by parents for parents: Tel: 0808 800 2222; www.parentlineplus.org.uk

Stepfamily helpline Scotland: Tel: 0845 1228655.

For more information on relationships, the legal differences between marriage and cohabitation and how to manage conflict in parental relationships, visit our family of websites:

www.marriedornot.org.uk
www.mymumanddadarguealot.org.uk
www.theparentconnection.og.uk

Single parent families

Gingerbread – A support organization for over 1.8 million lone parents and their children throughout England and Wales: www.gingerbread.org.uk

National council for one-parent families (merging with Gingerbread) – Currently they can help with childcare, employment, money issues, children's behaviour, useful organizations and more: Tel: 0800 018 5026 (Monday to Friday, 9 a.m. to 5 p.m.; Wednesdays, 9 a.m. to 8 p.m.); www.oneparent-families.org.uk

Other books of general interest

Deacon, Caroline (2002) *The NCT book of Breastfeeding for Beginners*, Thorsons.

Deacon, Caroline (2004) *Babycalming – simple solutions for a happy baby*, Thorsons.

Deacon, Caroline (2007) *Teach yourself Your Baby's Development*, Hodder Education.

Eliot, Lisa (1999) *Early Intelligence – how the brain and mind develop in the first five years of life*, Penguin.

Gerhardt, Sue (2004) *Why love matters – how affection shapes a baby's brain*, Routledge.

Goddard Blythe, Sally (2005) *The well balanced child – Movement and early learning*, Hawthorn Press.

Gopnik, Alison; Metlzoff, Andrew and Kuhl, Patricia (1999) *How babies think – the science of childhood*, Weidenfeld & Nicolson.

Stadlen, Naomi (2004) *What mothers do – especially when it looks like nothing*, Piatkus.

teach
yourself

feeding your baby
judy more

- Are you tired of 'gurus' and their menu planners?
- Do you want a healthy diet your baby will enjoy?
- Do you need help to cope with fussy eaters or tantrums?

Feeding your Baby is your sensible and realistic guide to everything a baby needs for a healthy, happy and balanced diet. From breast-feeding and weaning to the needs of the growing child, it has plenty of practical information on every area, with advice on healthy foods, support for mealtime battles and tasty recipes for all ages.

Judy More is the found of the Child Nutrition consultancy. Previously a paediatric dietician for several hospitals and community trusts, she now runs a private consultancy offering nutritional advice to parents and children.

teach yourself

green parenting
lynoa cattanach

- Do you want advice on natural pregnancy and birth?
- Do you want to be an environmentally aware parent?
- Would you like a happy, healthy and balanced family?

Green Parenting is a practical guide to making informed, ethically aware choices for your family. It covers all elements of domestic life, from children and nappies to travel and toys, offering step-by-step advice and useful suggestions for every level of interest and commitment.

Lynoa Cattanach is a director of BabyGROE, a charity promoting a parent-friendly approach to a greener life through its magazines and website.